TOTALLY BOOGIE WOOGIE

Simon Tyler

Southern House Publishing

ISBN: 978-1-9997478-0-0

www.tylermusic.co.uk

DEDICATION

To everyone who keeps the music alive.

CONTENTS

A Brief History

Boogie woogie is essentially an off shoot from the blues, and although they are closely related, they each have a distinct feel and style to themselves. It is hard to put an exact date on when the style first appeared, but it's generally considered to have first come about during the 1920's, although it could be argued that an undeveloped version of the music could have been heard a decade earlier. The blues is known to stem from America's deep south at around and about the turn of the century, boogie woogie developed from that, being blues based but going off in a different direction of its own.

The boogie pianists created the style over a period of time, being very much a child of its environment. The pianists in question would have been self taught, earning part of their living from playing in the barrel-houses. These were cheap drinking and entertainment establishments for the lumber and railway workers of the south. They would have been rough places, nothing more than wooden shacks where the African American workers would drink and dance with the piano for entertainment. It was in these sort of places that the musicians started to develop what we now refer to as boogie woogie, although the term 'barrel-house' music would perhaps have been used at that time. Later on, when some of the workers moved into the cities the music followed, and what became known as 'rent-house parties' came to be. These were hard times and the people would have been poor and often struggled to get by, one solution was to hire a pianist and charge people to come for the nights entertainment.

The music developed in these environments, in a sense becoming what it is by necessity, as it was created to suit a purpose. The pianists who played these venues could perhaps be compared to a DJ of today - supplying music to dance to. The pianos themselves would have been of poor quality, badly maintained and probably poorly tuned, this combined with the level of volume required to compete with the parties residents went towards shaping the music into what we now know. The pianists would experiment at these establishments (with an audience often too inebriated to be particularly critical or even care) and slowly over the years boogie woogie came to be.

The sound of the repetitive bass is often thought to have been influenced by the railways, with some songs even having the word 'train' within them. You can see why when you listen to some boogie woogie, as there is a resemblance to the sound of a train running on its tracks and the rhythm of the music.

The term 'honky tonk' is another you may have heard, sometimes used to describe an out of tune piano - honky tonk piano - which would have been the typical kind of instrument used at the time. But the term originally referred to a place where you had a drink and a good time. This included trains that took the American workers away for holidays, these were complete with drinking bars and were referred to as being 'honky tonk trains'. You may recognise this as being part of the title of the well known boogie woogie classic 'Honky Tonk Train Blues'. So you can see how the environment helped to shape the sound of the music, like many things, the environment we are in has a large influence upon us and music is no different here.

The actual term 'boogie woogie' is generally thought to have been first used by Clarence Pinetop Smith, when he recorded his song 'Pinetops Boogie Woogie' in 1928. The words boogie woogie were in both the title and the lyrics of the song, the term being used to describe how he wanted the listener to dance. The name must have caught on, as from this point onwards it become the standard term for the music.

Within the music industry you always have what you might refer to as 'fads'. Being the latest 'in' thing that everybody listens to for a time, until the novelty wears off and something new comes along, well boogie woogie was no different in this respect. The music developed at the turn of the century, becoming fully formed in the mid to late 1920's, it was extremely popular all through the 1930's, with interest hanging on well into the 1940's. But.. by the the 1950's people were moving on, with various forms of Jazz becoming popular and the early beginnings of rock 'n' roll appearing (which in turn had its day, it's the way of things). Nothing is forever, but fortunately - like most styles of music - boogie woogie still lives on.

It may not sell by the millions, but people still enjoy it all over the world. There are many modern exponents of the style that are here for us to enjoy, recording and performing. They keep the music alive, evolving it further to new levels, complete with new influences and ideas. But we should give thanks to the likes of Pinetop Smith, Albert Ammons, Pete Johnson and Meadelux Lewis, (to name but a few) as without them, we wouldn't have the music we know today.

An Introduction

I first discovered boogie woogie about twenty five years ago, and in truth it was quite by accident. I was a fan of Jerry Lee Lewis at the time, being impressed by his energetic and aggressive style. Unfortunately for me, this was at a time before the internet came to be (I'm showing my age a little here) so it was extremely hard - or close to impossible - to find any decent transcriptions of what he played. That and the fact that my piano teacher had no knowledge of this style of music, made it next to impossible to make a great deal of progress.

At some point I came across an article in a keyboard magazine, I believe it was called something along the lines of 'how to play rock 'n' roll piano'. At the time, I thought I had won the lottery (although yes, this was before the lottery was introduced here in the U.K). Finally, I had something to show me what was going on, the article was of course slightly limiting, but it still made a huge difference, allowing me to listen to the records and then do my best to imitate them.

What exactly has this got to do with boogie woogie I hear you say? Well it was the following month that the same magazine had another 'how to play' article, this time on something called 'boogie woogie'. What on earth is boogie woogie I thought, I'd never heard of it back then (remember... no internet), but I did notice that it had some similarity to the previous months article, so I was intrigued. I had some fun learning from the magazine, after all... rock 'n' roll and boogie woogie... it's all related. But that was it for a few years as I couldn't find anything else in the local shops to further my education. Those of you who grew up before the internet will understand what I mean, those who can't remember life without online shopping... you don't know how lucky and spoilt you are.

Sometime late I discovered a television show called 'Later - with Jools Holland', this became my favourite show for quite a few years and it's nice to see it's still going today. But what made it stand out for me was the pianist that hosted the show, being of course Mr Jools Holland. To put it mildly, I was blown away by his playing, I hadn't heard the piano sound like that before, the thing came alive at his touch. It was of course the same basic style of music I had come across before by accident, but after hearing what it can sound like, what a piano could sound like.. from that time on I was completely hooked!

So here I'd like to say a big thank you to Jools, for properly introducing me to this music. Of course, it was still hard to find any music notation to learn from – leaving me to learn mostly by ear - and it was this lack of books on the subject that has led me to be here now... I hope it's of some help.

How To Use This Book

Boogie woogie is very much an improvisational style, while you can just learn the songs that are available in sheet music, I believe that to truly enjoy playing this music you need to go further than this and learn how to improvise. Most of the best boogie pianists improvise all the time, they may have set pieces that they perform, but even these will often be played slightly different each-time. If you listen to the old classic recordings, you will also come across different various different versions of the same songs.

The simplicity of the style (along with the blues it's related to) is what makes it so ideal for improvisation. It's based on relatively simple chord progressions (normally twelve bars long) which consistently repeat themselves. There's nothing too complex to worry about, making it ideal to just relax and let go expressively and just enjoy yourself.

With this in mind, this book was created to help you learn to play and improvise, so it isn't and doesn't intend to be a song book in any shape or form. What it is intended to do is give you the building blocks of boogie-woogie, show you the structure, how it is formed, what is played by the left hand and then how to play the right hand over the top. I'll say now that you can't learn everything from a book, but it is a good way to start, once you have the basics under your belt you can continuously improve, by listening, copying and then experimenting (just like the originators did all those years ago), once you have the basics... the sky is the limit.

The book is split into sections. To start with, the structure of boogie-woogie is discussed with some of the elements that make it what it is. Then there is a section on the left-hand, this is initially kept separate and should be treated separately when starting out, as it is important to practice the left hand separately. The right-hand is split into sections, scales, chords and riffs etc, and I would suggest treating this separately to the left-hand initially too.

The layout of this book is perhaps not traditional, but then it isn't meant to be a walk through type (starting from page one and going through in sequential page order). Instead it is meant to be a resource of ideas and information. It is intended that you take what you need at any one time, practice and then go back for something new to work with (be it another bass line, or to learn a new scale). I feel that this arrangement is more practical and in keeping with the style of music it refers to. You are - after-all - essentially teaching yourself, this is here to supply you with the information you need, what you choose to learn and in what order... that's up to you.

BOOGIE WOOGIE
BASICS

Roman Numerals

To begin with, a quick explanation of the use of Roman Numerals, you may be familiar with this, but just in case, here it is.

What are they?
Roman Numerals are basically an old form of numbering.   (shown below)
I = 1   II = 2   III = 3   IV = 4   V = 5   VI = 6   VII = 7

These are a common way of expressing the chords used within a piece of music/song.

Why not just write the actual chords used?
The reason being is that they have the advantage of not being set in any one key, which then makes the transposing of songs (playing in a different key) an easier task. The use of these are common for jazz musicians and also for the blues, with classic songs being played in all manor of keys.

How do they work?
Each Roman Numeral (number) refers to a different degree of the scale.

(Shown here with the scale C Major)

You can see above which degree of the scale each numeral refers to.

So in the Key of C, a chord symbol with...

I = 1st degree of the scale = C chord.
III = 3rd degree of the scale = E chord.

Or in another Key (G for example)...

I = 1st degree of the scale = G chord
III = 3rd degree of the scale = B chord

If this is all new to you, don't worry, it's easy to get to grips with and will soon become second nature in no time.

The Structure Of Boogie Woogie

Boogie woogie is very closely related to the blues, so it also uses the same basic structure as traditional blues music. This generally means a repeating 12 bar chord progression.

The 12 bar blues structure predominantly uses three chords (in its most basic form). Those chords being from the Tonic, Subdominant and Dominant degrees of the scale. Or as they are more commonly referred to as... the 1st 4th and 5th degrees of the scale.

As we discussed on the previous page, when these are written down they are done so as Roman numerals, so we are looking at the I, IV and V chords, (1, 4 and 5).

An example of a basic 12 bar blues progression

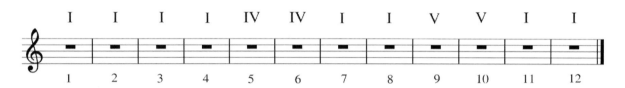

It consists of...

4 Bars of I   2 bars of IV   2 bars of I   2 bar of V   2 bars of I

(Example. 1   12 bars in C)   (I = C   IV = F   V = G)

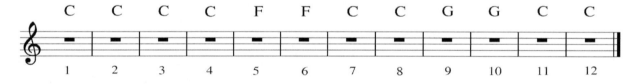

(Example. 2   12 bars in G)   (I = G   IV = C   V = D)

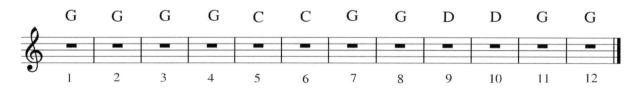

(Example. 3   12 bars in A)   (I = A   IV = D   V = E)

Variations

There are some simple but common variations to the 12 bar blues progression.

(Variation. 1)

This substitutes the V chord for the IV chord on bar 10.

(Variation. 2)

This substitutes the I chord for the IV chord on bar 2.

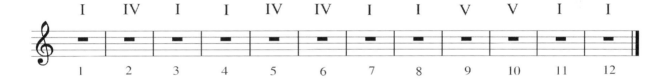

(Variation. 3)

This is a combination of both the above.

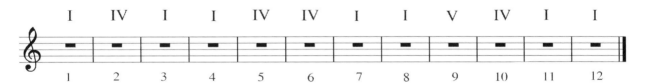

(Variation. 4)

This substitutes the V chord for a II chord in bar 9.
Not that commonly seen and only really works well with walking bass lines.

8 Bar And 16 Bar Progressions

Although the 12 bars is the most commonly used chord progression, there are also two other structures to know about, the 8 and 16 bar blues progressions.

(Example of an 8 bar progression)

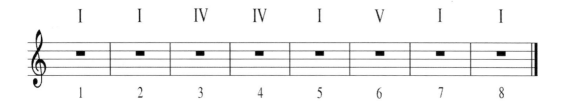

(Example of a 16 bar Progression)

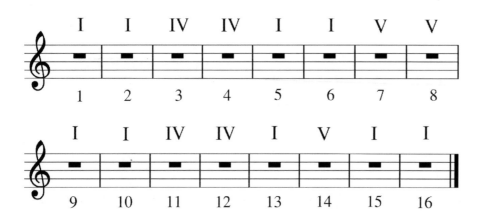

As you can see, the 16 bar chord progression has similarities to the 8 bar pattern. The last eight bars are the same as the eight bar progression, with the first eight bars varying slightly, with the last two bars of the V chord creating a feeling of building up to the second half of the progression.

Time Signature And Rhythm

You will find that boogie woogie will pretty much always be written in the common time signature of 4/4, sometimes written as a C (for common)

Having four beats per bar gives you eight possible eighth notes (quavers) per bar, these drive the rhythm along and is where the term 'eight to the bar boogie' comes from - which you may have heard in the past.

Example of eight to the bar (straight timing)

But, straight isn't how boogie woogie is normally played. It usually has a triplet feel, which is sometimes referred to as a 'swing feel'.

The best way by far to get the idea/feel of this, is just to listen to boogie woogie recordings.   Even play along to the record/CD, as copying is an excellent way to learn.

The Triplet Feel

When I say triplets, it means that each beat is divided by three (three notes per beat).

In the example bar below the first two beats are triplets, a single beat divided into three. So if you were to count the timing, there would are three counts to each beat.

As opposed to straight timing, where you would have either one, two or four notes per beat. You would count as shown in the bar below.

Unlike the straight timing, with a triplet feel you have an uneven number of notes. So there are three counts per beat.

Fortunately in boogie woogie this is quite easy to get to grips with as it is generally all played in triplet time, so you are not playing triplets over the top of straight timing. But just to confuse you... it is not normally written as it is played.

You will find boogie woogie written in several ways.

1. Written Straight

When written straight, it assumes you will 'swing' the timing yourself.

2. Quavers And Semiquavers

Probably the most common form (and used in this book) but not technically correct.

3. Written In Triplets

Technically the correct timing.

Strangely, although no.3 is technically the correct timing, it is rarely the way boogie woogie is actually notated as a whole. You may see small sections notated as triplets, but this will usually be when all three notes of the triplet are to be sounded.

So, both timing forms written below....

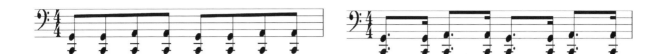

Actually mean this...

So when you see this written...

This is the actual timing you want to play.

And when you see this written...

This is the actual timing you want to play.

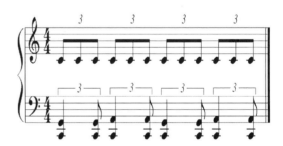

And when you see this written...

This is the actual timing you want to play.

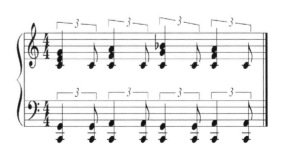

Typical Song Structure

A typical boogie woogie piece generally consists of several elements.

Introductions

Just like most forms of music, boogie woogie often has an introduction at the beginning. You don't always have include one, it is possible just to start pounding it out, but it's common to at least have a small lead in.

There are various ways you can do this, but the traditional way isn't to have an extra separate section added on to the beginning, it is to actually use the first four bars of the 12 bar sequence.

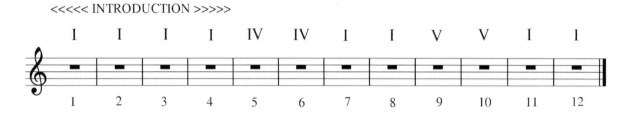

The first four bars of the I chord are replaced with the introduction and you then continue straight onto the IV chord.

Verses

After the intro the song will generally consist of a series of 12 bar verses. These normally have a theme to them, a repeating riff that can be varied throughout. More complicated songs will change the bass line used mid song, or even the whole feel of the piece before often returning to the original pattern.

Breaks

Sometimes you might have a break at some point (halfway perhaps), where the continuous rhythm takes a small break. (You probably have heard this when listening to the music). Often the left-hand stops while the right-hand plays something of interest. This does a good job of breaking up any monotony, it's not always done, but it's good to know about and then use when you feel it's appropriate.

Endings

All good things must come to an end and boogie woogie songs are no exception, traditionally these tend to be pretty short and sometimes sudden affairs, although there is no rule that says you can't create something more extravagant.

BASS LINES

The Backbone Of Boogie Woogie

Quite possibly the single most important part of boogie woogie is the bass line. I think the title of the book 'A left hand like god' sums this up quite nicely. In a sense, the left-hand is doing the job of both a drummer and a bass player (especially when played solo with no accompaniment). It sets the rhythm, the tempo and the feel, without a good strong and solid left-hand, a boogie just won't woogie (or something like that).

The idea of this chapter is to show you a variety of possible bass lines, although it is by no means all encompassing, it will get you started. Some are quite common, some not so much and others are simple variations. The more left-hand patterns you know the better, as it allows you change and vary the music and so keep it interesting - to those who might listen and to yourself.

When learning this style, by far the best way to practice is to learn the bass-line first, by itself and separate from any right-hand melody etc. Being an improvisational style it's essential that the left-hand becomes pretty much autonomous, as when this happens it frees you up to then improvise over the top with the right-hand. If you have to think too much about the left when playing with both hands, then things will probably fall apart to some degree.

So when you learn a new left-hand pattern, practice it over and over and over again, until it is pretty much automatic, like it's almost part of your left-hand, with a life of its own. This isn't quite as bad as it sounds, as the patterns tend to be only one or two bars long. The bass patterns can be varied of course, even changed completely through the course of a song, but individually they are quite short and so easily memorized.

The feel is very important, the previous chapter mentioned the 'swing feel' and it is important to get this, otherwise the music won't sound right. I suggest you listen to the masters as much as possible, as hearing the music regularly will help imprint this feel into your brain and allow you to replicate it far easier, as you can not really learn the feel from music notation.

Just remember, a flamboyant right-hand can't make up for a weak left-hand, so practice, practice, practice.

How To Use This Section

It's not practical to learn all of the bass pattern straight away, so I would suggest that you choose one or a few (it's up to you) and then concentrate on them until you are happy. The bass lines are also shown in a 12 bar progression and obviously it needs to be practiced as such, also... don't forget to practice these in different keys. Although you will need to become fairly proficient at transposing to learn in new keys, I have included the bass lines in all twelve keys in the appendix at the end of the book. Hopefully this inclusion may help/encourage people to learn in different keys, which is important to do.

Practicing to a metronome is not a bad idea at times, this will help you keep your timing tight, which should then carry over to when played without. It is very important to make sure you have the feel right and that the timing stays tight, these are very important points to focus on.

Some boogie-woogie is extremely fast, others a little more sedate (perhaps played with a little more expression/feel), but regardless, don't necessarily try and play the patterns at lightning speed straight away (depending on your own currant ability of course). Speed is really a by-product of accuracy, you can't effectively play a piece fast until it's ingrained on your subconscious. So start off at a pace where you can play accurately and then with practice you will naturally be able to speed things up without any problems.

Fingering

Each bass pattern has some fingering suggestions.You by no means have to use these, although options are normally fairly limited. I must point out that these will not work in all keys, but they are a good basis to start from. I would suggest to always play them as you feel most comfortable, remember, this isn't anything like classical music with strict rules of right and wrong, if it feels good... it probably is.

Note... regarding finger numbering, thumbs are counted as number one.

One point I will add is that sometimes (depending on hand/finger positioning) when I use the fifth finger (little finger), I often also use the fourth finger on the same key (both fingers being on the one key). I did this naturally without thinking – it. This might sound strange, but it does help reinforce the weaker fifth finger helping to create a stronger bass - although it isn't always possible - depending on how the rest of the hand is positioned. If you find this is comfortable or it comes naturally to you too (and some pianists do play this way) then don't worry, if it works... use it.

Bass Line 1

This left hand bass line is often referred to as 'the chop' or a 'chopping bass'.
If you only ever learn one boogie woogie left hand pattern, then I'd say that this is probably
THE one to learn. It's simple enough and if you've been listening to
the music you'll probably recognize it straight away.

(Fingering Suggestions)

The first example is perhaps more sensible, although many pianists use the second example. I seem to switch between the two. Use whichever feels most comfortable.

(Shown as a 12 Bar Blues Progression)

Bass Line 2

There are numerous variations of the basic 'chop' pattern.
The one shown here includes the use of the seventh.
This can be used by itself or intermixed with the basic 'chop'

(Fingering Suggestions)

I would suggest the first example, as the use of the extra finger will make it less tiring to play. But use whichever feels most natural.

(Shown as a 12 Bar Blues Progression)

Bass Line 3

This further variation of the basic pattern makes use of the third and flatten third.
This can be used alone or mixed with other variations.

(Fingering Suggestions)

Personally I play this like the second example. Try them both and decide.

(Shown as a 12 Bar Blues Progression)

17

Bass Line 4

This variation adds an extra root note an octave above creating a chord.
As a point of interest, a chord consisting of octave roots and a fifth is referred to as a power chord by guitarists (although not considered a true chord in the classical sense) and it does live up to its name, adding a little bit of extra power to the sound.

(Fingering Suggestion)

Being a chord based pattern the options of how to play are fairly limited. I would suggest the first example unless you have larger hands.

(Shown as a 12 Bar Blues Progression)

Bass Line 5

This is quite a subtle variation of the previous pattern.
It starts off essentially the same, but holds the last notes of one bar over to the next.
This can be used on its own or intermixed with the previous version.

Try to emphasize the last two notes tied over between bars and the
root note which is played immediately after.

(Fingering Suggestion)

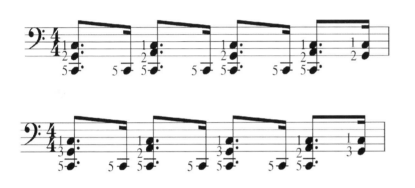

Being a chord based
pattern the options
of how to play it are
fairly limited. I
would suggest the
first example as I
find it less of a
stretch than using
the third finger.

(Shown as a 12 Bar Blues Progression)

Bass Line 6

This variation is quite interesting as it includes a kind of walk up on the second bar. You could incorporate various walk ups with this pattern, making it quite interesting to play around with.   (See section on Walk-Ups)

(Fingering Suggestion)

> I would suggest playing this as shown, it uses octaves all the way through, so may be more difficult with smaller hands.

(Shown as a 12 Bar Blues Progression)

Bass Line 7

This variation of the 'chop' uses the same notes, but they
are played differently to create a different feel.
Notice how the root is held over onto the following beat, this creates a
slightly laid back feel compared to repeating the note again.

(Fingering Suggestion)

As with most of the 'chop' type patterns, how you play will depend on if you have a preference of using your thumb over the second finger. This pattern isn't too tiring to play with the root note being tied over.

(Shown as a 12 Bar Blues Progression)

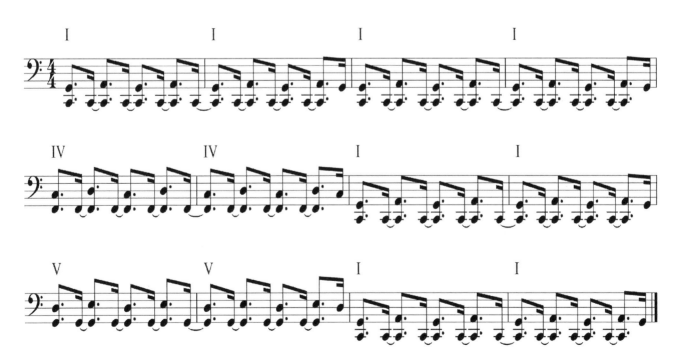

Bass Line 8

Although most of the left hand patterns have no names to speak of, I've heard of this one being referred to as a kind of inverted chop, and you'll probably see why once you've had a look at it.

(Fingering Suggestions)

Note the way the third and minor third are played with the same finger (Although this common technique isn't possible in all keys).

(Shown as a 12 Bar Blues Progression)

22

Bass Line 9

This subtle variation of number eight plays the root note on every eighth beat, which makes it a little stronger, although perhaps a little more energetic to play.

(Fingering Suggestions)

This pattern is perhaps harder physically (due to the root note being quite repetitive.
(played twice per beat)

(Shown as a 12 Bar Blues Progression)

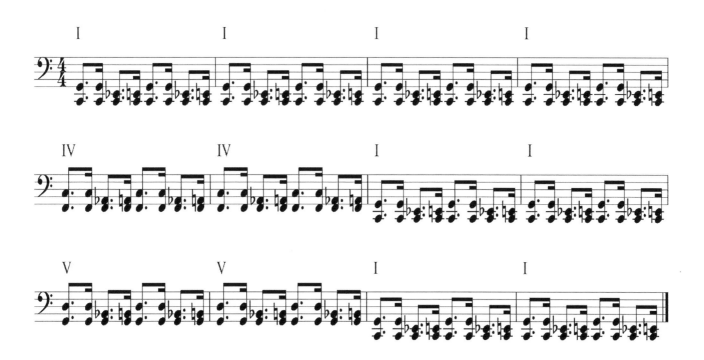

23

Bass Line 10

This is a well known left hand pattern, although it has several variations.

(Fingering Suggestions)

> Using the third finger is probably more sensible Although you may find using the second is more comfortable.

(Shown as a 12 Bar Blues Progression)

Bass Line 11

This variation of the pattern includes a couple of chords, which creates a fuller sound.

(Fingering Suggestions)

This is quite hard in the physical sense. A good left hand in boogie woogie takes consistent practice to build up the necessary left hand strength.

(Shown as a 12 Bar Blues Progression)

Bass Line 12

This further variation differs with the omission of the 4th.

(Fingering Suggestions)

> Your preference on
> the use of finger two
> or three will decide
> how you play this.

(Shown as a 12 Bar Blues Progression)

Bass Line 13

Another more chord based variation.

(Fingering Suggestions)

Your preference on the use of finger two or three will decide how you play this.

(Shown as a 12 Bar Blues Progression)

Bass Line 14

This variation uses a descending pattern, which can be used quite nicely
in conjunction with the previous patterns, 10 - 12.

(Fingering Suggestions)

Both fingering options
shown work quite well,
or use a combination
of both. Whatever
comes naturally to you.

(Shown as a 12 Bar Blues Progression)

Bass Line 15

This version is similar, having the same basic notes as before, but they're arranged in a different order.

(Fingering Suggestions)

Both fingering options shown work quite well, or use a combination of both.

(Shown as a 12 Bar Blues Progression)

29

Bass Line 16

This is a relatively simple pattern, although sometimes they work best.

(Fingering Suggestions)

> A choice of either the second or third finger, whichever you feel is the most comfortable. Or combine the two as you feel fit.

(Shown as a 12 Bar Blues Progression)

30

Bass Line 17

This bass pattern can also be found in rock n roll, with what
could be described as a shuffle feel.   Often heard being played at a fast tempo,
but you can also slow it down for a more laid back feel.

(Fingering Suggestions)

It's a choice between using the second finger or also including the third. Here the first option is perhaps more sensible with less movement of the thumb. Although personally I tend to play it the second way.

(Shown as a 12 Bar Blues Progression)

Bass Line 18

A variation of the previous pattern, which continues walking its way
upwards to the seventh, instead of just repeating the same one bar.
This could be used on its own, but probably better utilized
in-conjunction with the previous version.

(Fingering Suggestions)

I tend to use the
second example,
but you might
find the first less
tiring to play, as
more fingers
equals less overall
hand movement.

(Shown as a 12 Bar Blues Progression)

Bass Line 19

While this pattern may well look very similar to the previous one, it
should actually sound quite different when played with the right feel.
The previous pattern is often played at a high tempo,
but this one works best at a slower speed..
Try to emphasize (accent) the second beat (root and third) and perhaps the
last note of each bar that carries over (the fifth).

(Fingering Suggestions)

I tend to use the
first example, but
you might find the
second less tiring
to play, more
fingers here
equals less overall
hand movement.

(Shown as a 12 Bar Blues Progression)

Bass Line 20

Another variation on a theme.
Starting with single notes and ending with a couple of thirds.

(Fingering Suggestions)

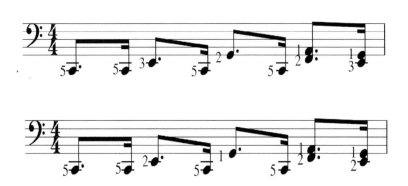

> I tend to use the
> second example,
> it's simpler, which
> makes it easier to
> my mind, but the
> choice is yours.

(Shown as a 12 Bar Blues Progression)

Bass Line 21

This variation includes the use of the minor third.

(Fingering Suggestions)

Note the use of the
same finger coming off
the minor third and
onto the third.
(Not possible in all keys)

(Shown in a 12 Bar Blues Progression)

35

Bass Line 22

This version of the pattern adds the flattened 9th, which gives a dissonant, almost dirty sound that almost growls at you. The effect lessens the faster it is played, so personally I prefer to use it at a more sedate tempo, but it works either way.

(Fingering Suggestions)

If you play this pattern at a relatively slow pace, then it becomes more important to accent the off beats (2+4) as the effect is more pronounced than when playing at a fast tempo.

(Shown as a 12 Bar Blues Progression)

Bass Line 23

This variation of the previous pattern still includes the 9th for that gritty
sound, but then moves upwards to include the seventh.
You could use this by itself, but it will work best when combined with others.

(Fingering Suggestions)

> There's not too many ways to play this, as the thumb has to
> travel so far up, while finger five must remain by the root.

(Shown as a 12 Bar Blues Progression)

37

Bass Line 24

This is really a variation of the chop, it replaces the root and sixth with the third
during beat two, a small change, but it creates a different sound.
Try to empathize beats 2 and 4 slightly to bring out the feel.

(Fingering Suggestions)

Your preference
of either finger
two or three will
dictate which you
prefer. Both
work equally well.

(Shown in a 12 Bar Blues Progression)

38

Bass Line 25

This pattern has notes tied over into the second bar, the end of which should also be tied over again into the first bar of the repeated pattern.

(Fingering Suggestions)

The first example using the third finger is probably less tiring, due to there being less hand movement overall.

(Shown in a 12 Bar Blues Progression)

Bass Line 26

This pattern is a single bar that walks upwards while alternating with the root note.

(Fingering Suggestions)

Your preference of either fingers two or three will dictate which suggestion you prefer Both work equally well.

(Shown as a 12 Bar Blues Progression)

Bass Line 27

This single note pattern walks downwards with an up-turn at the end.

(Fingering Suggestion)

A choice of using
either the third
or the fourth finger.

(Shown as a 12 Bar Blues Progression)

Bass Line 28

This left hand pattern should be relatively well known.
The octave stretch might be tricky for those with smaller hands.

(Fingering Suggestion)

Slightly unusual in that all five fingers are
employed with this left hand pattern.

(Shown as a 12 Bar Blues Progression)

42

Bass Line 29

Works best at a medium tempo and in conjunction with the next pattern.

(Fingering Suggestion)

There's not too many ways to play this, as the thumb has to
travel so far up, while finger five must remain by the root.

(Shown as a 12 Bar Blues Progression)

Bass Line 30

This is a simplified variation of the previous pattern, which can work well when used in conjunction with the previous one.

(Fingering Suggestion)

There's not too many ways to play this, as the thumb has to travel so far up, while finger five must remain by the root.

(Shown as a 12 Bar Blues Progression)

Bass Line 31

This left hand pattern should be played at a relatively slow and relaxed pace, as opposed to the usual more frantic boogie, which can make a nice change.

(Fingering Suggestion)

There's not too many ways to play this, the only practical way employs finger two on the fifth, leaving your hand in a set position.

(Shown as a 12 Bar Blues Progression)

Bass Line 32

This is quite a popular bass line, it is generally played at a slower, more relaxed pace than most boogie woogie, so play at a nice easy tempo and enjoy.

(Fingering Suggestion)

Use whichever you find most comfortable. This probably depends on the size of your hands

(Shown as a 12 Bar Blues Progression)

Bass Line 33

As you can see, this pattern consists of triads (3 note chords).
Because of this try not to play too low down, as it will sound very muddy.

(Fingering Suggestion)

You could substitute the second finger for the
third on beats two and three if you prefer.

(Shown as a 12 Bar Blues Progression)

Bass Line 34

This is a variation of the previous pattern, but employs a four
note chord instead with a single note tied over.

(Fingering Suggestion)

> Again you could substitute finger two for finger
> three in places - if it feels more comfortable to you.

(Shown as a 12 Bar Blues Progression)

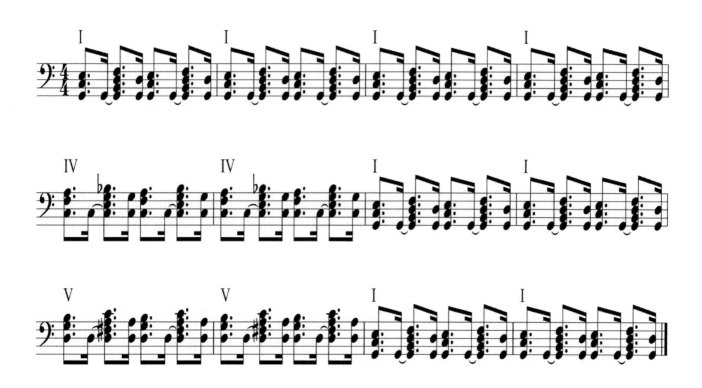

Bass Line 35

This is another subtle variation on the same theme as the previous pattern.

(Fingering Suggestion)

> There's not too many ways to play this, as the thumb has to
> travel so far up, while finger five must remain by the root.

(Shown as a 12 Bar Blues Progression)

49

Bass Line 36

This pattern is quite a busy one, going up and then down chromatically, while alternating with the root note below.

(Fingering Suggestion)

(Shown as a 12 Bar Blues Progression)

Bass Line 37

This is an extended version of the previous pattern, which could be used on its own or in-conjunction with the shorter version.

(Fingering Suggestion)

(Shown as a 12 Bar Blues Progression)

Variations Combined

While the left-hand patterns shown can be used on their own, a song or improvisation normally varies or combines the left-hand patterns together, as this is more interesting than consistently repeating the same one or two bars.

Example. 1   If you take the basic chop type pattern...

It has some variations you can use...

1.

2.

3.

4.

In the following examples the basic pattern will be used for the main basis of the left-hand, with either one or two other patterns used to vary it through the twelve bars. This is often done at the point of chord changes, as it emphasizes the change and kind of helps build to it and also prepares the listener for it.

Example. 1a

Note the use of pattern fig.1 at the changes...
from I to IV (bar 4)   IV to I (bar 6)   V to I (bar 10)

Example. 1b

Note the use of pattern fig.1 and 2.
Fig 1. Bars 4,6 and 10.
Fig 2. Bars 2,5,8 and 12.

Example. 2 Take the inverted type chop pattern...

You could use this with these (for example) …

1.

2.

3.

Fig 1. Bars 9
Fig 2. Bars 10
Fig 3. Bars 4,6 and 12

Note the use of the IV chord on bar 10.

Example. 3

You could use this with the following (for example) ...

1.

2.

3.

Fig 1. Bars 4 and 8
Fig 2. Bars 9 and 11
Fig 3. Bars 6 and 10

Example. 4

You could also use this with the following (for example) ...

1.

2.

3.

Fig 1. Bars 4,8 and 10
Fig 2. Bars 6 and 12

Example. 5

This could be nicely incorporated with...

1.

2.

Fig 1. Bars 4,6 and 12
Fig 2. Bar 10

The Walk Up

The walk up (as we will call it) is pretty much as it sounds, you walk the bass upwards. This is done just before the chord changes and is a nice introduction to the next chord, also working well as a lead up to a change in the right hand melody, it's very effective.

In a typical 12 bar blues progression, it would be used on the fourth bar leading into the IV chord on the fifth bar.

Example 12 Bars (I To IV)

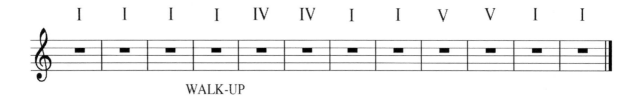

Below is a typical walk up played as alternate octaves.
It starts on the root, jumps to the $2^{nd}/9^{th}$ and then moves up chromatically, ending just one semi-tone below the root note of the next chord.

(A walk up in a 12 bar blues progression)

Variations (Walk-Up)

Variations of ways you could walk up.

1.

2.

3.

4.

5.

6.

Obviously different versions will work better
with different bass lines, learn them all and experiment,
find out what works best in what situation.

Further Variations

(I To V)

You can also use a walk up on bar eight, leading into the V chord - although this isn't heard as often as the I to IV version.

Example 12 Bars

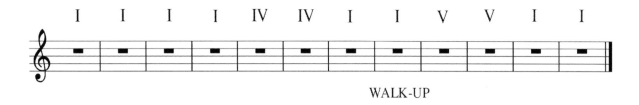

WALK-UP

Here you start on the root again, but then jump to the 3rd and move up chromatically to one semi-tone below the root of the next chord.

(V To I)

It is also possible to walk up from the V chord, back to the root chord.

Example 12 Bars

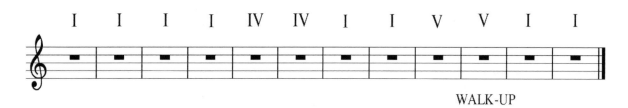

WALK-UP

This starts on the root, then jumps to the 2nd/9th before moving up chromatically to one semi-tone below the root of the next chord.

The Walk Down

What goes up, must come down... so you can also walk downwards if you wish.

(Positions Of Possible Walk Downs)

(IV To I)

1. Walking down from the IV to the I chord.

2. Variation (IV down to to the I chord).

(V To I)

1. Walking down from the V to the I chord.

(I To V)

1. Walking down from the I to the V chord.

Example 24 Bars

This includes a left hand pattern that in itself consists of a walk up,
plus variations of both walk ups and walk downs.

Practice, repeating until it becomes second nature.
Incorporate walk ups with other bass lines you are working on.
In time (with listening to recordings) you will get the feel of what works.

Walking Bass

If you have been listening to boogie woogie, then you have most likely heard examples of what is referred to as a 'walking bass'. It isn't specific to boogie woogie as such, and variants are found in blues and jazz music, but there are differences between them all. The term 'walking' stems from how it kind of walks up and down the keyboard/scale.

Example

Above is a walking bass line in perhaps its simplest form.
As you can see, it walks upwards and then back down.
This example pattern consists of the 1st 3rd 5th and 6th degrees of the scale.

(Fingering Suggestions)

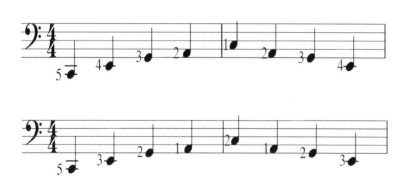

If you have large hands, you could approach this like the first example. Personally I would use something more like the second example, as crossing over will allow for further freedom of movement, up or down.

While you can play a walking bass with single notes, in boogie woogie it's common to use octaves more often than not.

(Fingering Suggestion)

Due to the stretch, these octave based patterns would normally be played with fingers 1 and 5.

Starting Out...

If this is new to you, then I would suggest learning/practicing the walking bass in small steps. (Obviously feel free to ignore this if you are more advanced)

1. Start with a simple single note walking pattern.

Practice playing this through a standard 12 bar chord progression.

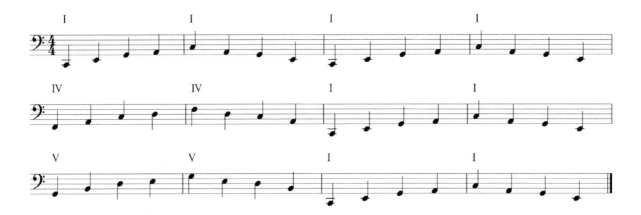

2. Then practice playing in octaves, alternating between the two root notes.

Practice this again through a standard 12 bar chord progression.

3. Put the two together to create a typical boogie woogie type walking bass.

Practice playing this through a standard 12 bar chord progression.
Once you have this under hand, you'll have a nice boogie woogie walking bass.

(A Note On Practice)

Initially, practice at a slow speed, don't make the mistake of trying to play this fast straight away.
Speed is a by-product of accuracy, so if this is new to you, don't rush it.
Practice at a slow to moderate pace. As you become more accomplished over time, you will naturally be able to speed up.
Once you have a basic walking bass under your hand, you can then start to experiment with variations.
One of the fun things about playing a walking bass is it's fluidity, it can change constantly as you play, remaining a repetitive pattern if you wish, or you can alter it to whatever comes to your mind.

Walking Bass Examples

Some example walking bass line patterns.

1.

This is probably the single most common walking bass pattern within boogie woogie. Using alternating octaves, it follows the same pattern as on the previous page.

Degrees Of Scale Used
1 – 3 – 5 – 6 – 1 – 6 – 5 – 3

2.

This follows the same basic pattern, but steps up to the 7th (dominant, not major) instead of going up to the higher root note.

Degrees Of Scale Used
1 – 3 – 5 – 6 – 7 – 6 – 5 – 3

Included are the walking bass lines shown as degrees of the scale. Knowing what you are playing - in terms of its position within the scale - helps greatly when it comes to transposing to other keys. When you know your scales, it's then easier to think, 1, 3, 5 etc... and so easily work out what to play in another key.

3.

On this shorter pattern, you walk up to the fifth via the flattened 5th.

Degrees Of Scale Used
1 − 3 − 4 − 5♭ − 5 − 4 − 3 − 2

4.

A simple pattern using only the root, third and fifth.

Degrees Of Scale Used
1 − 3 − 5 − 3 − 1 − 3 − 5 − 3

5.

Interesting pattern that includes the sixth, seventh and ninth.

Degrees Of Scale Used
1 − 2 − 3 − 2 − 1 − 7 − 6 − 5

6.

Relatively short pattern - works well with patterns seven and eight.

Degrees Of Scale Used
1 – 7 – 6 – 5 – 1 – 7 – 6 – 5

7.

Emphasizes the minor third - works well with patterns six and eight,

Degrees Of Scale Used
1 – 7 – 6 – 5 – 3♭ – 3 – 3♭ – 3

8.

Version of number seven that walks back upwards.

Degrees Of Scale Used
1 – 7 – 6 – 5 – 3♭ – 3 – 5 – 6

9.

Walks down via the seventh and up via the sixth.

Degrees Of Scale Used
1 – 7 – 6 – 5 – 1 – 3 – 5 – 6

10.

Essentially the same as the first pattern, but it's reversed – first walking downwards and then back upwards in the second bar.

Degrees Of Scale Used
1 – 6 – 5 – 3 – 1 – 3 – 5 – 6

11.

Simple alternating octaves, creates a break from the more complex patterns.

Degrees Of Scale Used
1 – 1 – 1 – 1 – 1 – 1 – 1 – 1

12.

A slightly more complex pattern.

Degrees Of Scale Used
1 – 7 – 6 – 5 – 5♭ – 4 – 3♭ – 3

13.

This is a version of the first pattern, but uses fifths (intervals) to create a fuller sound.

Degrees Of Scale Used
1 – 3 – 5 – 6 – 1 – 6 – 5 – 3

14.

This is an alternate version of number thirteen, but the reverse way round.

Degrees Of Scale Used
1 – 3 – 5 – 6 – 1 – 6 – 5 – 3

Walking The Bass

We have already covered a selection of walking bass patterns, but to create an authentic sounding bass you have to combine these and improvise further, creating what is hopefully a fluid and evolving bass line.

Example. 1

Here you have 12 bars of a walking bass pattern.
On bars 4, 6 and 10, you walk up to the 7th instead of the the root.

Example. 2

Here you have the same basic pattern but this time bars 2, 8 and 10 walk up to the 7th.
On bars 11 and 12, the pattern walks down instead.

Example. 3

Here the twelve bars walk up to the 7th on bars 2 and 6.
But bars 9 and 10 use a different shorter pattern and swaps to the IV chord on bar 10.

Example. 4

Here the twelve bars start off using a mix of patterns from numbers one and two.
But bars 7 and 8 use a different pattern again – from pattern nine.

Example. 5

Here, on the last two bars (11 and 12) it changes to different pattern.

Example. 6

The main pattern used (pattern three) has a slight variation on bar 8 which leads onto the V chord. This uses simple alternating octaves, which then steps down to the IV chord, which in turn steps down to lead back to the I chord, and the original pattern.

Example. 7

Here it starts the same as the previous example, but bars 3 and 4 continue to walk upwards (which is repeated on bars 7 and 8). Bars 9 and 10 use a shortened version.

Example. 8

Here the main bass pattern is a one bar example, but on bar 4 it changes to walk up to the IV chord. On bars 7, 8, 11 and 12 it uses a longer version of the pattern.

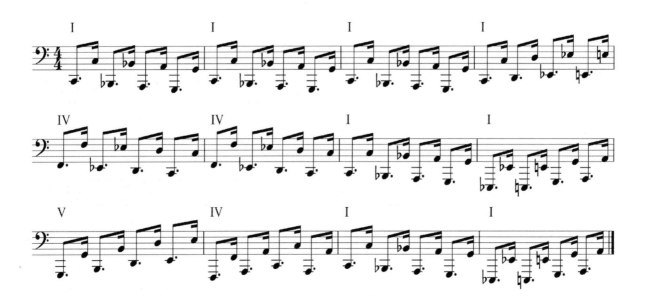

Example. 9

Here we have another bass pattern - from pattern five.
On bar 4 you have a short walk up to the IV chord.
Bar 9 uses octaves in an alternating pattern, walking back up to the I chord.

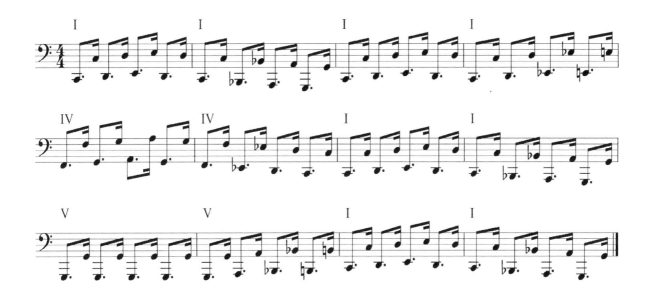

Example. 10

This example shows how you can move up and down the keyboard rather than staying within the same register (it uses the pattern from thirteen).
Bars 1 and 2 start off on one octave, but bars 3 and 4 walk down an octave lower.

Example. 11

This example is a slight departure in that it uses the II chord on bar nine to walk up to the V chord on the following bar.

Example. 12

This is to give an example of how much a walking bass line can move around.
It also includes an unusual VI chord on bar eight as well as the II chord on bar nine.

These examples are not meant to be a complete guide, but hopefully they should give you an idea of some possibilities. Take what you see and experiment with it, listen to recordings and try and recreate what you hear with the building blocks that you have learnt.   Most of all... enjoy it.

RIGHT HAND
ELEMENTS

Introduction

Once you have the basics of the left-hand it's time to look at the right-hand. If you think in terms of a band, the left-hand is much like the drummer and bass player, where as the right hand is perhaps a combination of rhythm and lead guitar. So although the right-hand can be melodic, boogie woogie was originally considered as dance music, so the right-hand is also very rhythmic.

The right-hand can consist of either simple rhythmic chord patterns or more complex melodic riffs. Both of these are repeated over the twelve bars, normally with some degree of variation, with the next twelve bars being different again, or maybe a modified version of the former patterns.

Individual right hand riffs are interchangeable with the left hand patterns, so once learnt they can be used - or modified - over and over again in different situations. So the key is to learn as many as you can, the larger your repertoire the better and more varied your improvisations can be.

To Be Covered

● Scales

● Chords

● Embellishments

● Riffs/patterns

● Introductions

● Turnarounds

● Endings

This book is intended to be a resource of information rather than a step by step guide, with this chapter outlining the elements that go into the right hand. There is no correct order to go through, so pick out whatever you feel is most relevant to you. Improvising is really a case of experimenting, based on the knowledge that you have learnt. - scales/riffs. A basic improvisation consists of any left-hand with the riffs you know played over the top, simple as that. Of course it takes time to become comfortable enough to do this, but learn as many riffs/patterns and scales as you can, as it's this knowledge that allows you to experiment and create something new, which is what makes this style so enjoyable to play.

The Scales

Although boogie woogie is - technically speaking - relatively simple in its structure, in order to improvise it will help greatly to know some scales. You can learn to play from song books without any such knowledge, but it's the improvisation that makes this style such a joy to play and knowing these will help you to do so.

You may already know all your scales, in which case skip right past, but if not, don't worry, thankfully there isn't too much to it.

What Is A Scale

A scale could be defined as being a set of notes ordered by frequency (pitch) in either an ascending or descending order.

The notes of a scale are numbered by their steps up the scale (referred to as degrees). The first note of the scale (the key note or root) would be referred to as the 'first degree' and the second note as the 'second degree' and so on.

The first scale to learn here is the major scale.

Major Scale

The degrees of the scale are numbered in an ascending order as they move upwards. Technically there is only seven notes in a major scale, as the eighth note shown is merely the first degree repeated, but one octave higher.

Although the major scale isn't normally used in Boogie Woogie, it would be a good idea to familiarize yourself with it, as it will help your understanding of scales in general.

Major Scale In 12 Keys

You may well know your scales, but just in case... here are the 12 major
scales for you to familiarize yourself with before moving on.
Sharp keys are not included, as for our purposes
D♭ is essentially the same as C sharp etc.

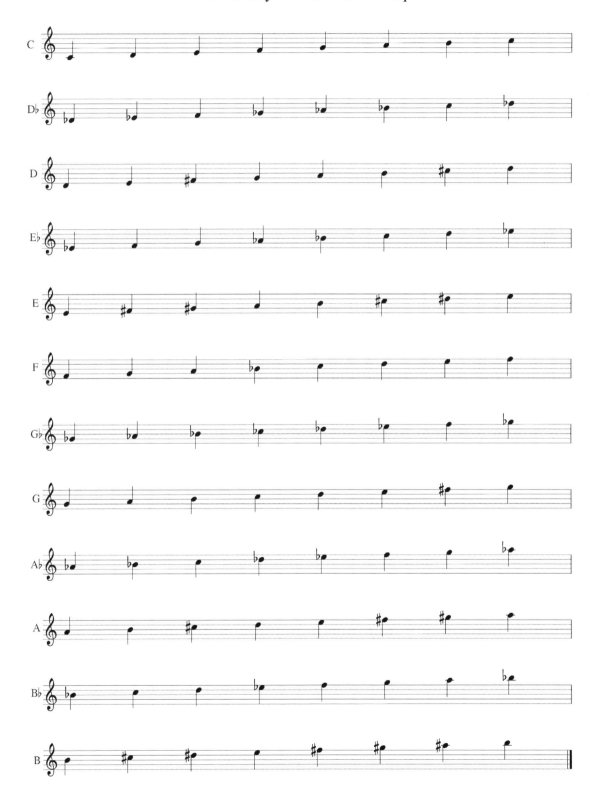

Boogie Woogie Scales

Despite the title above, boogie woogie doesn't actually have its own scales as such. The scales used to improvise are the same as those used within the blues, so what you learn for one style carries over nicely to the other.

It would be true to say that you can learn to play well by just memorizing riffs and patterns, but it will help immensely to know these scales. The thought of this may be off putting for some and if so, don't worry, just take your time and learn them slowly, don't punish yourself practicing relentlessly. Instead, practice them a little at a time, this way you will learn without getting tired of doing so, yet over time they will eventually become second nature.

We've already gone over the major scale - mainly as background information - but it doesn't actually work within this style due to its inclusion of the major seventh.
So... we have to look at the pentatonic scales.

Pentatonic scales are (as their name implies) only five notes in length.

The pentatonic scales are widely used in popular music and span various styles, including... variations of folk music, rock, country and the blues to name but a few.

Major Pentatonic Scale

The pentatonic scale is often used within popular music, it's useful to know, both for general knowledge and also because it's related to the blues scales.

It consists of the first, second, third, fifth and sixth degrees of the major scale.

Major Pentatonic Scale In 12 Keys

Familiarize yourself with the major pentatonic scales, they may be
quite simple, but they are very useful to know.

Major Blues Scale

The major blues scale is essentially the major pentatonic scale, but with the simple addition of the flattened third. This might not sound like much... but this 'blue note' transforms it.

Just like the major pentatonic scale, it consists of the first, second, third, fifth and sixth degrees of a major scale, but the addition of the flatten third changes it, opening it up and giving it a blues feel (the flattened third often being referred to as a 'blue note').

The major blues (just like the major scales) has a relative minor scale. For example, the C major blues scale uses the same notes as the A minor blues scale.

If you have played some boogie woogie before, then you might notice how some of the right-hand riffs and patterns you already know fit nicely within this scale.

When you practice the scale (or any scales) it is a good idea to not always start and end on the root, try going from the second degree to the second, or the third to the third. This helps when improvising, as you wont necessarily be starting from the root.

Examples Below

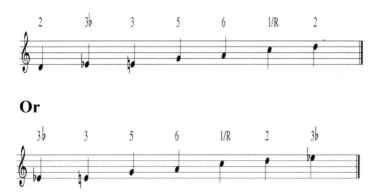

Or

Fingering Suggestion

The choice of using finger 1 or 5 on the last note depends on if you're ending, reversing, or repeating the scale again on the octave above.

Major Blues Scale In 12 Keys

Practice them until they become second nature.
Try to play the scales ascending and descending and over
more than one octave (two or three).

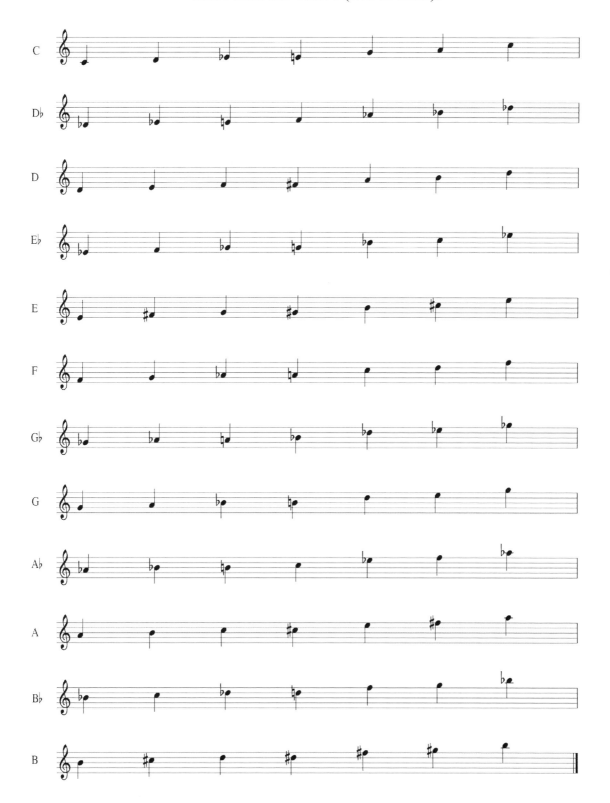

Minor Pentatonic Scale

The minor pentatonic scale is shown below. It consists of the First, flattened third, fourth, fifth and flattened seventh degrees of a major scale.

When you practice the scale (or any scales), it is a good idea to not always start and end on the root, try going from the second degree to the second, or the third to the third. This helps when improvising, as you wont necessarily always be starting from the root.

Examples Below

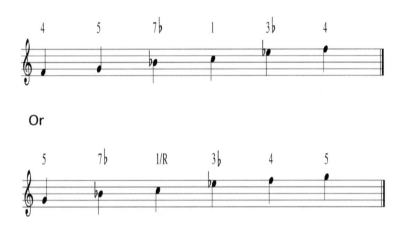

Or

Fingering Suggestion

Several ways to to play this, below is just a suggestion. Being a pentatonic scale the fingering from major scales doesn't really transfer as it involves less fingers. The 5 or 1 at the end depends on if you are ending or continuing the scale.

Minor Pentatonic Scale In 12 Keys

Practice them until they become second nature.
Try to play the scales ascending and descending and over
more than one octave (two or three).

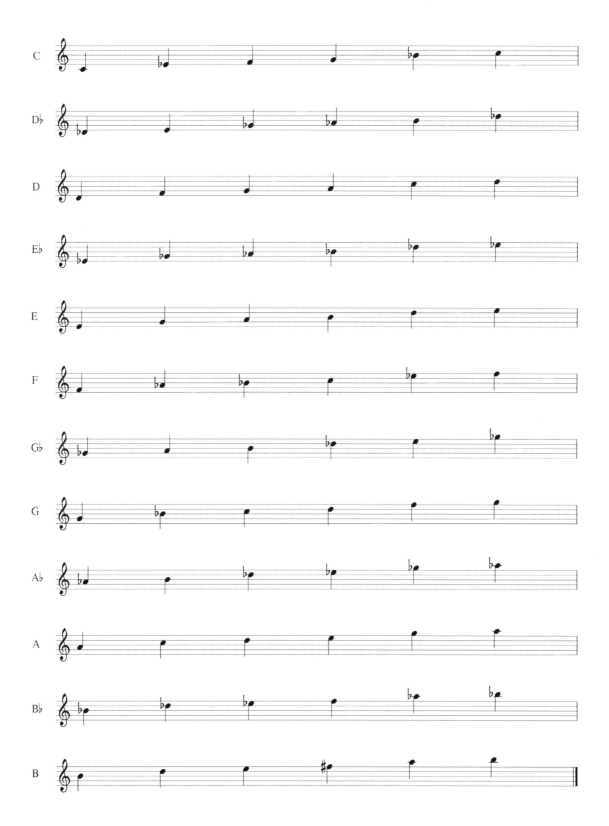

Minor Blues Scale

This is probably the most commonly known scale used within blues and boogie woogie. Referred to by many as simply... 'the blues scale'.

It consists of the minor pentatonic scale, but with the inclusion of the flattened fifth. This might not sound like much of a difference, but with the 'blue notes' being included it creates what is probably the definitive blues sound.

It consists of the first, flattened third, fourth, flattened fifth, fifth and flattened seventh of the major scale.

When you practice this scale (or any scales) it is a good idea to not always start and end on the root, try going from the second degree to the second, or the third to the third. This helps when improvising as you wont necessarily be starting from the root note.

Examples Below

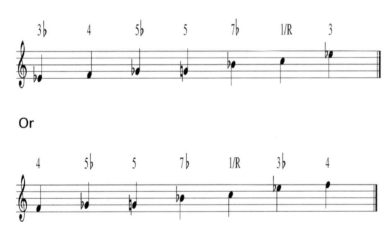

Or

Fingering Suggestion

There are other ways to play this scale and the fingering will differ in some keys, but this is one example.

Minor Blues Scale In 12 Keys

Practice them until they become second nature.
Try to play the scales ascending and descending and over
more than one octave (two or three).

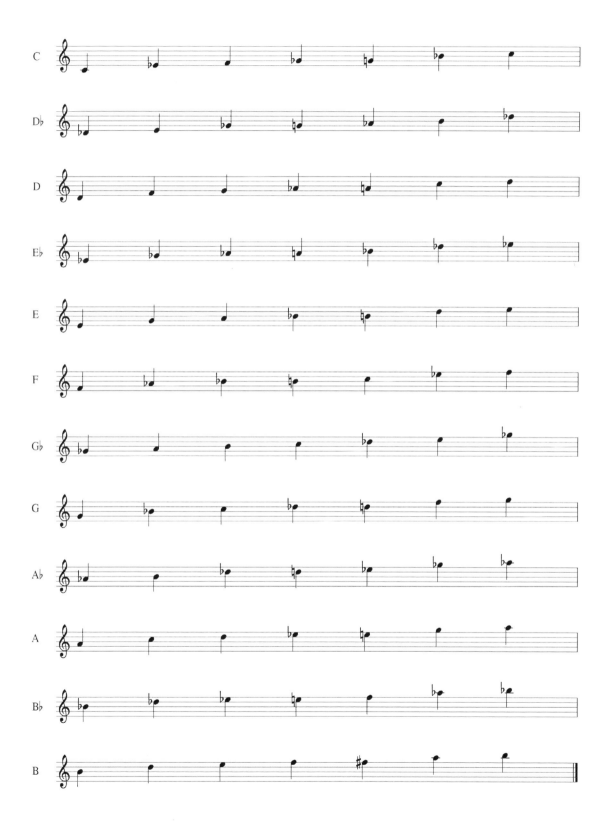

Combined Blues Scale

This isn't an official scale as such, but it's worth mentioning as you may find it useful. Some blues pianists (including some well known ones) look at the scales in a slightly different way, they combine them into one, creating a single pool of potential notes to chose from while improvising.

It pretty much consists of every note, but leaves out the flattened 9th/2nd and of course the major 7th.

Now, I will point out that this isn't really meant for running up and down as it is shown. It's more like a list of the possible options from which you can choose from. Some of these are best used simply as passing notes, or to create dissonance before resolving to a more pleasing sound.

The chord tones here being C, E, G and B♭ (1,3,5,7♭) could be considered the key destination notes, or those that you would resolve to.

Notes D, E♭, F and A (2,3♭,4,6) could be considered more as passing notes with G♭ and A♭ being even more dissonant.

So this combined scale can be looked upon as your complete vocabulary, kind of like all the tools in your tool box, or the ingredients in your kitchen. I wouldn't recommend only learning this scale, as it's not officially a scale, but you may find its addition useful.

I always feel that rather than following a rule book... experimenting yourself (playing around) is the best way to learn what actually works and where, your ears will tell you.

Combined Blues Scale In 12 Keys

Practice them until they become second nature.
Try to play the scales ascending and descending and over
more than one octave (two or three)

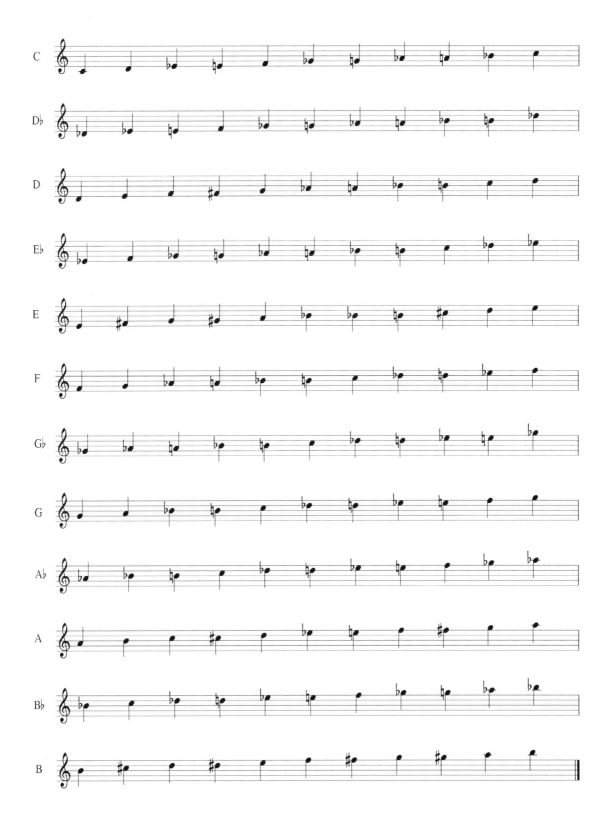

Regarding Scales For I, IV And V

The blues and boogie woogie are quite unusual in how the scales work over the chords. Obviously when you play either the I, IV and V chords, you can use its own corresponding scale over each chord.

So when (for example) you play a G chord... you can use a G scale.

All pretty normal and perhaps obvious, but...

In the blues you can also play the 'I' scale over all three chords (I, IV and V).
This does go against standard music theory, but it's what makes the blues the blues.

> **(Examples)**
> In the Key of C, the C scales will work over all C, F and G chords.
> In the key of G, the G scales will work over all G, C and D chords.

Try the example below to see what I mean.

1. Uses a C scale over all I, IV and V chords.
2. Uses the corresponding keyed scale over each chord.

1.

2.

Scale/Chord Table

The table below shows which key/scale works over which chords.
Either the chords own corresponding scales or the scales from the 'I' chord.

Key	Scales For I Chord	Scales For IV Chord	Scales For V Chord
A	A	A or D	A or E
B♭	B♭	B♭ or E♭	B♭ or F
B	B	B or E	B or G♭
C	C	C or F	C or G
D♭	D♭	D♭ or G♭	D♭ or A♭
D	D	D or G	D or A
E♭	E♭	E♭ or A♭	D♭ or B♭
E	E	E or A	E or B
F	F	F or B♭	F or C
G♭	G♭	G♭ or B	G♭ or D♭
G	G	G or C	G or D
A♭	A♭	A♭ or D♭	A♭ or E♭

Chord Change Trick From I To IV

When you need to change from the I chord to the IV chord, a simple trick to remember
is just to simply flatten the third to create the next chord. As the example below shows
(key of C) flattening the 3rd from a C6 creates an F9 chord, which is idea for the IV chord.

Third flattened

Chords For Boogie Woogie

While it's fair to say that boogie woogie with its blues progressions is technically fairly simple in its structure (using I, IV and V in its simplest form). The actual chord within can be quite varied, including the use of... Major, Minor, sevenths, ninths, thirteenths, diminished, augmented chords and more...

We shall quickly cover how these chords are formed, before moving on.
All examples are in C, showing the chord and its make up within the scale.

Major Chords

A major chord is a triad, so called because it is made from three notes.
It is created from the first, third and fifth degrees of a major scale.

Minor Chords

A minor chord is made from the first, flattened third and fifth notes of a major scale.
Or... simply flatten the third of a major chord.

Diminished Chords

A diminished chord is created from the first, flatten third and flattened fifth of a major scale. Or... simply flatten all the notes of the chord apart from the root.

Augmented Chords

An augmented chord is created from the first, third and sharpened fifth of a major scale. Or... simply sharpen the fifth of a major chord.

An augmented chord is quite commonly used on the V chord in a blues progression (occupying bars 9 and sometimes 10 of a standard 12 bar Blues) it's also commonly used on the V chord within a turnaround.

Sixth Chords

A sixth chord is created from the first, third, fifth and sixth of a major scale. Or... simply add a sixth to a major chord.

Seventh Chords

A seventh chord is created form the first, third, fifth and flatten seventh of a major scale. Or... simply add a flatten seventh to a major chord.

(NOTE)

When the word seventh is mentioned within blues or boogie woogie, it refers to the dominant seventh (or flattened seventh) rather than a major seventh.
The major seventh doesn't work, try playing it and you will see what I mean.

Ninth Chords

A ninth is created from the first, third, fifth, flattened seventh and ninth of a major scale. Or... add the ninth to a seventh chord.

As you can see, a ninth chord consists of five notes, making it impractical to play in its complete form, so it is usual for a note to be left out (obviously not the 9th).

Flattened Ninth Chords

A flattened ninth chord is created from the first, third, fifth, flattened seventh and the flattened ninth.   Or... simply add a flattened ninth to a seventh chord.

As with a ninth chord, omit a note to make it a four note chord, the root is common. While it's a great sounding chord, it has quite a dissonant sound, so careful use is required.

Thirteenth Chords

A thirteenth chord is created from the first, third, fifth, sixth and flattened seventh. Or... add the sixth to a seventh chord.
Again, although it is physically possible to play the chord in its entirety, it is usual to leave out a note and play it as a four note chord. For perhaps obvious reason, the sixth and seventh shouldn't be left out, as it would no-longer be a thirteenth chord.

Chord Positions

Always remember when improvising that all chords have several different inversions available, so try not to get stuck with using chords in just one position.

The first position would be referred to as the 'root position', with the root on the bottom.
The next would be the first inversion, with the root moved to the top.
Then the second inversion would move the third to the top... and so on.

Examples Of Different Chord Inversions (Shown in C)

Major

Minor

Diminished

Sixth

Seventh

Tremolos And Trills

You may have heard both these terms before, but what are they?
They are in fact very similar, but not quite the same thing.

Trill

A trill is when you play rapidly, alternating between two notes, fluttering between the two. These are either a half step apart (one semi-tone) or a whole step at most.

Tremolo

A tremolo is when you play rapidly, alternating between notes that are further apart. This can also be two notes or three or four (chords).

Within boogie woogie, such fluttering between two notes is normally further apart than what defines a trill, so it is the tremolo that is generally used, although not always. It is common thing to see in blues and boogie woogie and a useful tool to learn, as it turns the playing of a relatively dull chord into something quite interesting. Thirds are often used for tremolos, or fifths, sixths or any chord you can think of.

Examples of how a tremolo might be written.

The C and the E shown here would be played quickly, alternately.

Any thirds within the scale you are using are fair game for a tremolo.
A couple more examples shown below.

Tremolo With Octaves

Tremolo With Fifths And Sixths

Tremolo's using fifth and sixth intervals. Note that when you use a sixth interval, the notes are the same as if you were to play thirds, but rearranged.

Tremolo With chords

These can generally be seen written in two different ways.

1.

2.

Grace Notes Or Slides

A grace note is an extra note that is added in front of an existing note. It is generally considered to be melodically and harmonically non essential, being thought of as more of an embellishment. Some may refer to these as a slide note, as you are sliding from one key to another and this also possibly refers to the guitars ability to slide notes.

It is said that within blues music, pianists started to use grace notes as an alternative to the guitars ability to bend notes (obviously not possible on the piano) this does make a lot of sense, as it is the closest you can get to emulating that effect. While the official definitions state it is non essential... I beg to differ when it comes to this kind music, for me it is an intrinsic part of the sound.

You might see a grace note written like these below.

The grace note has no time value of its own, timing wise it is part of the main note.
It is played extremely quickly, like a stepping stone to the main note.

The most common notes to use are the minor (flattened) third and minor (flattened) fifth, as these are considered among the 'blue notes'.

How these are played varies as to which key you are playing in.
If you look at the key of C (example below) then you will see that the notes directly below the third and fifth are black keys. This makes it easy, as you simply slide off the black key (grace note) and onto the white key (main note) all with the same finger.

If you was in the key of A (for example).
Then the note directly below the third is a white note, making it impossible to slide upwards from one to the other with one finger. In this case you have to use two fingers.

Rolls

What I describe as being a 'Roll' (others may have another name for this) is essentially a very fast arpeggio, using either the scale or sometimes just the actual chord you are playing. It creates an effect that is not dissimilar to a tremolo, but still quite distinct in itself. The use of this is very common in blues and boogie woogie and you would without a doubt have heard these on recordings. You should learn and practice them as they are a good tool to add to your collection.

Example. 1

This is basically a four note arpeggio, the four notes of the chord (in this case a C9) are played in the space of half a beat.

Example. 2

This has the same timing as the first one, but shows an upward motion.

In this example, you would probably use the same finger for both the F♯ and the G, sliding from one to the other.

Example. 3

This shows a downward motion, but this time with five notes per half beat.

In this situation, you would still only use four fingers, the B♭ and the A being played by the same finger, sliding off from one and on to the other.

Arpeggios

An arpeggio is only a short roll downwards over one chord (as opposed to the continuous rolling sections shown previously). You might see them written like the example below.

Glissandos

A glissando is when you slide your fingers up or down the keyboard from one note to another. The effect is much like running your fingers across a harp and striking all of the strings.

It has been used by many people in various styles, but it's probably Jerry Lee Lewis who is most famous for its use. The term itself originates from the French word 'glisser' which means to slide.

They are written like the example below.

They are used in boogie woogie, but not too often. They are good way to get peoples attention and sound quite impressive, but shouldn't be over used, less is definitely more. They are simple in theory, but still take plenty of practice to play well. It's considered best to use the nail side of your fingers (nails are obviously harder than skin) to slide along the keys (up or down) but careful, it can still damage you.

(NOTE)
A good tip to doing these well, is to not be chaotic or haphazard in their execution.
Have a definite starting point and a destination in mind, this creates a far better,
cleaner sound, otherwise they can become a little messy.

LEFT AND RIGHT COMBINED

Chord Ex.1

To get started with the right-hand, lets begin with a very basic vamp type pattern.
Below shows a major chord played on the beat (beats 1 and 3). Simple enough.

Shown below with the timing.

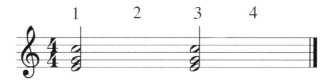

Now try playing this with both hands together, the left-hand playing a 'chop' type pattern
through twelve bars in the key of C.

Chord Ex.2

On/Off Rhythm

This pattern uses the same major chords, but this time it has an off/on rhythm.
This gets its name, because the first chord is played 'off' the beat and the second is
directly 'on' the beat.

To create the right feel, it is important to get the timing right. The first chord is played
just before the next beat. It will coincide directly with notes on the left-hand, so if you
play them together the timing becomes easier.

(Timing shown below in true triplet form)

Chord Ex.3

This example uses different a pattern, which is on/off the beat.
The timing is shown below, but again each major chord coincides with a note in the
left-hand pattern, which makes the timing easier.

(Timing shown below in true triplet form)

Chord Ex.4

Here we are introducing more chords.

I chords are 6ths	C6 (C major with an A)
IV chords are 9ths	F9 (F major with E♭ and G)
V chords are 7ths	G7 (G major with an F)

Also note that in the chord positions used, the 'I' chord only requires a single note to drop a semi-tone to create the IV chord, a nice easy change.

Chord Ex.5

The 12 bar example below shows how you can play these chords in different positions and on different octaves of the keyboard.

109

Chord Ex.6

Here the pattern has slightly different timing to the others, you may find this trickier to begin with, but once you have the feel of it you will be fine.
This pattern wouldn't be used consistently, but rather used for a bar or two to vary things up a little.

Shown below is the timing over the top of a left-hand pattern, playing them together will make it easier to get the feel of it, with the slight syncopation through beats one and two. All shown in triplets in order to make it easier to read.

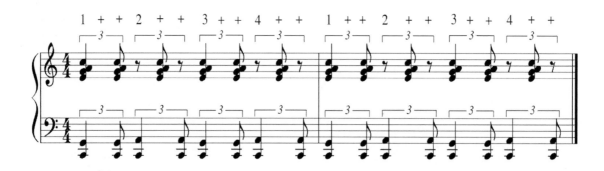

You could also vary the timing a little to mix things up, as shown below.

Shown with the left-hand.

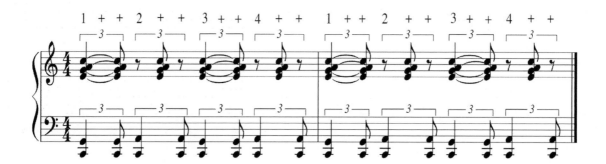

Chord Ex.7

While just using straight chords in a simple vamp is fine, you can also add a little something to it. The 12 bar example below shows a simple chord pattern with a couple of notes linking the bars together, this includes the minor third (flattened third) one of the 'blue' notes.

Note the use of sixth chords this time on all but the V chord.

Chord Ex.8

Chord Ex.9

The 12 bar example below shows a simple chord pattern with a
single note at the end of the bars that links them together.
Sometimes a single note can be more effective than many notes.

Chord Ex.10

This is 24 bars made with a combination of different patterns.

Continued...

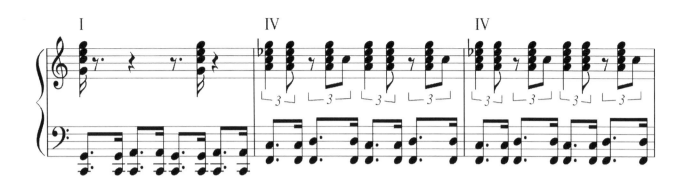

Chord Ex.11

Another 12 bar example showing a similar pattern, but with altered timing.

Chord Ex.12

A variation with a different left-hand and a tremolo.

Chord Ex.13

This example shows the use of some simple chords over a walking bass.
Often the more complex the left-hand, the simpler the right-hand can be.

Practice With Different Left Hand Patterns

The examples so far obviously don't cover every possible bass line, so don't forget to practice with different left-hands, as the independent nature of each hand means that riffs are interchangeable between most left and right-hand patterns.

Using 12 bars, practice different left-hands with various right-hand rhythmic patterns. Also... try this in different keys (important).
Experiment with the examples below, create your own, and also try playing what you hear from your favourite records.

Example. 1

Example. 2

Example. 3

Example. 4

Example. 5

Example. 6

Right Hand Riffs

Boogie woogie is often referred to as being an ostinato style, essentially being made from many different riffs/licks/patterns that repeat and change.

Basic improvising begins with learning and memorizing as many patterns/riffs as you can, as having a large repertoire is essential to keep the music varied and to give you the knowledge to enable the creation of your own.

So firstly we have some example right-hand patterns to give you a solid working basis, that will allow you to put your own boogie-woogie's together.

When you learn a new riff/pattern, it is a good idea to then transpose it into other keys. In an ideal world you'd be able to learn and know everything in every single key, quite a task, but definitely make a start in the right direction.

Examples

1.

2.

3.

4.

29.

30.

31.

32.

33.

34.

35.

36.

53.

54.

55.

56.

57.

58.

59.

60.

67.

68.

69.

70.

71.

72.

73.

Both Hands Together

Once you have some right-hand riffs under your belt, it's
time to put them together with the left-hand.

EX.1

This is the simplest version of the twelve bar progression, with a simple
right-hand pattern that repeats throughout.

> Notice how the entire twelve bars consist essentially of just two bars.
> The same pattern is repeated throughout but transposed to
> suit each individual chord.

EX.2

This is the simplest version of the twelve bar progression, with a simple right hand pattern that repeats throughout.

On the V chord (in this case a G) the right hand pattern was transposed to the G.
But...
Note how on the IV chord (in this case an F) the pattern wasn't transposed.
Instead all that changed was the 3rd was flattened.
This simple alteration changes the pattern to work with the different chord.
It in fact creates a 7th chord for the IV chord (F).

EX.3

Apart from just transposing the same pattern to the different chords, you can instead make small changes to the same pattern.
Shown here on the second bar.

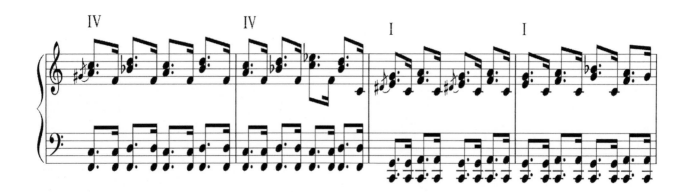

EX.4

Here we change the V chord on bar 10 for the IV chord and use
bars 9 and 10 to create further variations of the same pattern.

It is the V chord (starting at bar nine) that the entire twelve bar progression builds
up to. It starts on the I chord, hints at something different on bars 5-6 with the
change to the IV chord before going back to the I chord, which then prepares you for
the V chord. The last two bars set you up to repeat the whole thing, sometimes using
a turnaround (see later chapter).
So the point being, it's sometimes good to create something different on the V chord
(bar nine) as the whole twelve bars builds to it, so give them something.

EX.5

136

EX.6

Here you have several elements combined, the beginning pattern which then moves into a short chord vamp with a different part over the V chord.

EX.7

25 Bar Boogie

Here you have a slightly longer example - two twelve bar sections - that shows how on the following twelve bars you might change to a pattern that although different, compliments the previous one.

Continued...

139

EX.8

Turnarounds

A turnaround is a passage at the end of the twelve bars that is designed to lead into the next section of the song - being another twelve bar sequence. It isn't always used in boogie-woogie (probably more prevalent in blues) but it can still be used to good effect, but don't over use them. I would suggest that you learn as many variations as you can lay your hands on as you don't want to sound too repetitive with these.

As shown below, you can see the turnaround inhabits the last two bars of the twelve bars.

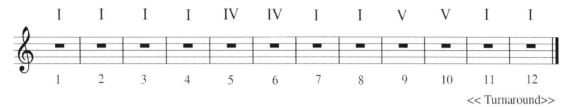

Example Turnarounds

1. This simple example only uses the last bar, where it steps up to the fifth (using octaves).

(Some examples including the right-hand)

2. This example walks downwards in the first bar, before stepping back up to the fifth.

Or

(Shown with the right-hand)

3. Here you have the reverse of the previous one, walking upwards in the first bar, it then steps up to the fifth once again.

Or

(Shown with the right-hand)

These examples will give you the basic idea, but there are so many ways
to play turnarounds that the best way to learn once you have
the basics, is to listen to recordings and copy what you hear.

EX.9

Here you have two twelve bar sequences joined together with a basic turnaround.

Notice the turnaround type pattern at the end?
The same patterns can be used to create an ending, although
you are then working towards the root instead of the fifth.

EX.10

EX.11

EX.12

EX.13

149

EX.14

EX.15

Introductions

Although you can just jump straight into a boogie woogie, it sometimes works better if you have an intro (introduction) to lead into the song. These can be very short and simple, or quite long and extravagant, or leave them out altogether... the choice is yours.

The most common/traditional way is to use the first four bars of the first twelve bar passage for the intro, after which you then go straight onto the IV chord on bar five.

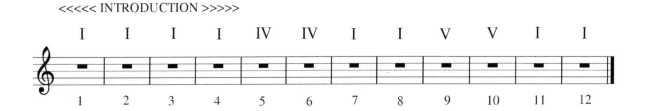

Examples

1.

2.

3.

4.

5.

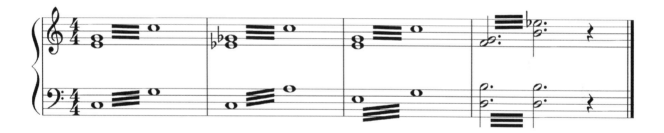

6.

7.

8.

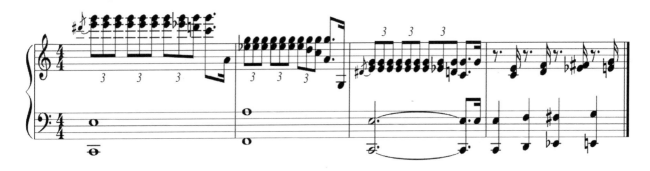

9. Here you have a six bar intro, that will lead into the seventh bar.

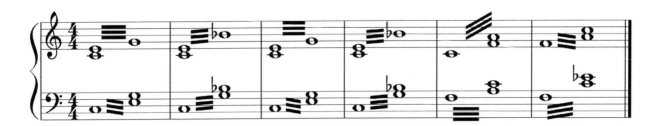

You don't of course have to stick with the same formula as shown.
If you listen to various recordings you will hear all kinds of different ideas, some of them are quite extravagant. Jools Holland's intro to 'River Boogie' on his 'Solo Piano' album is a great example of a longer intro, consisting of around thirty bars. This is well worth a listen and shows that there are no real rules, if it sounds good then it probably is.

Endings

All good things come to an end and boogie woogie is no different here. Much like the intros they can be short and sweet (like most of the old classic songs) or they can be longer more extravagant affairs.

Traditionally they take the place of the last two bars of the twelve bar sequence. This is of course the same position as the turnarounds, but then many endings are quite similar to the turnarounds, but instead of leading to the fifth, they work towards the root.

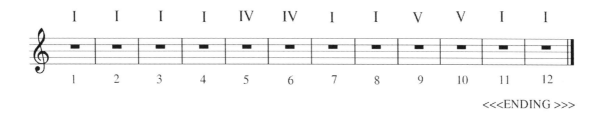

(Examples of basic endings)

Or you can use a turnaround based ending

4. This is very much a typical blues turnaround.

5.

6. Here we have the last chord held for over a bar, also note it's a good idea to end on an interesting chord, a sixth or a ninth perhaps.

7. Or here, where the right hand is dominant.

8. Here it has been extended further, with the inclusion of a slide up (glissandi) over four octaves, ending with a chord played over the two extremes of the keyboard.

9. Here you have a ninth chord played in a staccato manner and held at the end.

10.

There is no set rule on how to end a boogie woogie piece, it can be sudden or drawn out, dramatic or quite simple. When improvising it's up to you to decide what you feel will best suit what you are playing. As always, the best way to get a feel for this is to listen to the greats play as often as possible. Once you learn the basic tools, you will be able to copy what you hear on the recordings.

Breaks

You will have heard what I mean by this when listening to boogie woogie recordings. It's sometimes found around or past mid way of a song. It's kind of like a break in the action before the usual onslaught continues again. Usually the left-hand takes a break, sometimes completely, other times it just plays sparsely, leaving the right-hand to play. Occasionally you can hear the same thing reversed, with the bass taking a kind of solo, although this is not so common.

Below shows you the normal position of this within a twelve bar progression.

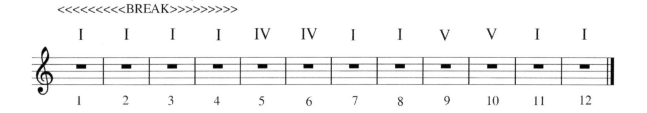

As you can see, it normally consist of the first four bars (much like an into).

Typical chords used for this might be...

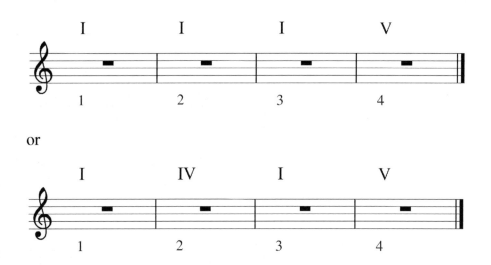

The chords follow the normal options for a blues/boogie, but on the fourth bar you tend to use the V chord, much like you would at the end of a turnaround. Although unlike a turnaround - that leads back to the I chord - here you follow on from the V to the IV chord, to then continue with what remains of the twelve bar progression.

Example. 1

A strong bass note is commonly played at the start of each bar.

Example. 2

Example. 3

This example has no left-hand until the last bar, it also uses the IV chord on the second bar.

> **(NOTE)**
> It's recommended to accent the bass notes in the left-hand,
> they should be particularly strong when played.

Improvising With Single Notes

Sometimes less is more, and in music the simple parts can often work even better than the more complicated ones. In boogie woogie, single note riffs work well and this kind of thing lends itself extremely well to improvising. Once you learn the relevant scales to the chords being played, you have your arsenal of notes to chose from.

Consider the scales you have at your disposal, these show you the possible notes.

(Key of C)

Major Blues

Minor Blues

Combined Scale

Knowing the scales/notes you have at your disposal, listen to your favorite music and pick out the parts you wish to know. The single note nature makes them far easier to work out than the more complicated riffs.

Remember, it doesn't matter if you can't quite get an exact copy of what you hear, it doesn't have to be. You have still learnt another riff, which potentially could be even better than the one you was trying to copy.

Beyond this, try inventing your own, play around with the notes that you know will work together, there are only so many to choose from. Experiment with different combinations and timings, see what you come up with and bare in mind... the old originators of the music did the very same thing.

Example. 1

Example. 2

Example. 3

Example. 4

Example. 5

Example. 6

Example. 7

Example. 8

Example. 9

Example. 10

Example. 11

Example. 12

Example. 13

Example. 14

Example. 15

Example. 16

Example. 17

Example. 18

Single Note Runs

There will be times when you want to run up an octave or two, or maybe even from one end of the keyboard to other, this can be accomplished quite simply by using the scales. While directly using the scales (note for note) can sound a little tiresome if over used, it's an easy way to move up and down the keyboard and can sound quite effective.

Example. 1

An upwards run covering four octaves using the C minor blues scale.

Or reversed going downwards.

Example. 2

An upwards run covering four octaves using the C major blues scale.

Or reversed going downwards.

Variations

There are many ways you can use the scales to run up and down the keyboard. Shown here are some examples of how you could group together notes from the scales into different runs.

Example. 1

Example. 2

Example. 3

Example. 4

Example. 5

Basic Song Template

The length of a boogie woogie is entirely up to you, there is no set formula. The example below is just that, an example. The intro is optional, the turnarounds are optional and shouldn't be over used. The break at the beginning of the fourth verse is optional, and you could extend or shorten the song to suit yourself, again.. there are no real rules.

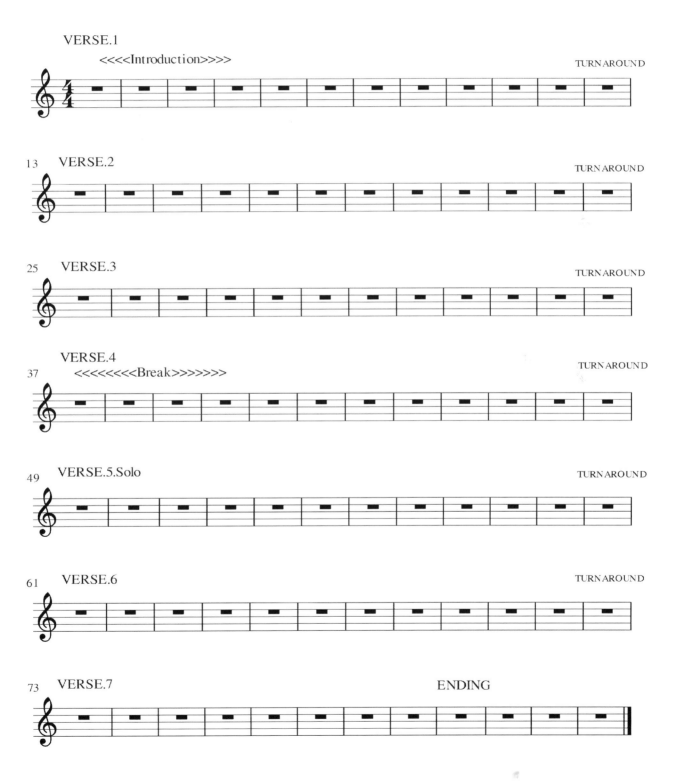

Example Improvisation

4

5

172

OTHER STUFF

APPENDIX

Tips On Practice

The subject of this chapter may seem obvious, but there are different ways in which you can practice the piano, some being more effective than others. Some things here are more specific to boogie woogie, but most of it is quite general.

How Often

This is a common question, heard by teachers everywhere, how often should you practice. I guess you could answer this in several ways, but I'll begin by answering it with another question... How good do you want to become?

Your brain is much like a computer, to do something it needs to be programmed. Now of course we don't work from computer coding (at least not yet) so to learn something new we need to actually do the thing in question, repeating it over and over again, there is no short cut.

So it simply comes down to how keen you are and perhaps more importantly... how much spare time you have to commit to practice. Obviously the more time you put in the better you get and in a shorter time frame. As an example, some professional classical pianists practice for eight hours a day, great, but for people who aren't full-time musicians this isn't exactly practical.

So I would recommend that you practice as often as you can (an hour a day is a nice stand point if possible) but only to the point where you are enjoying yourself. If it becomes tiresome then I think you're probably over doing it, and after-all, playing music is supposed to be fun, so don't ever lose sight of that.

When To Practice

You are of course probably busy with the rest of your life, work, family, other pastimes, so it is often a case of fitting in practice around everything else. But I will say, that if you are keen... then MAKE time to practice. It may be easy to say, but lets face it, most of you (if you try) can make an effort to factor in a small amount of time (most days) for a little piano time.

Another interesting point is that you don't always need to have very long sessions. An hours practice is... an hours practice. It's fine if that's a full hour, two half hours, or four quarter hour sessions, it's still an hour where you have concentrated on your music. So while you're waiting for that taxi or for the takeaway to arrive, have a quick ten minutes, it's very much worthwhile as it all adds up.

One thing that I used to do - during the week, was to set the alarm to wake up a little earlier, get up and have a quick practice in the morning before work. This worked brilliantly, as that time in the morning didn't interfere with other aspects of life, plus it split your practice up into a morning session and an evening session. These seemed like a life-time apart, which helped to stop you feeling like you're living on the piano and so helping maintain your enthusiasm. The only real down side was of course... waking up earlier.

Another interesting point regarding the time of day when you practice is to do with how your brain functions. Studies have shown that when you sleep soon after practicing your uptake of information is improved. This makes sense if you look at it logically, your brain is hard at work making new pathways, so to sleep soon afterwards (and sleep is where your brain does whatever it does to refresh itself) would seem to make sense. I don't expect you to have cat naps during the day, but a quick practice at night would seem to make sense if this study is true.

Also, I believe little and often can often be better than one long session. Of course, if you have lots of time spare then sure, sit down for a few of hours (I know I do) but your brain can only absorb so much at any one time (and this is the same with anything) so with that in mind it is probably more efficient to practice for a shorter time, but more often. Of course, we can all only do what we can fit in, when and where it's possible.

Strength And Stamina

Playing the piano isn't something that people tend to think of as being physical, and sure, it doesn't compare to power lifting or running a marathon. But it can be quite physically challenging for your hands (especially at higher levels). Imagine that classical pianist I mentioned earlier, practicing eight hours a day, without a doubt, that would put a strain on their hands and require a degree of strength and stamina that isn't present naturally.

Boogie woogie is generally a fast, energetic style of music, so naturally it is hard on your hands. The consistent pounding left-hand patterns particularly require a lot of stamina, And that stamina required to play well and consistently for any period of time... well, that takes time to build up. I know that if I have a period of time where I don't play at all, then I can feel it when I go back to the piano and try to play as usual. This isn't an issue if you practice often, you will gradually build up the strength/stamina and stay at that level. But just bare in mind that to keep that strength in your hands you need to keep the playing regular and consistent. On the flip side of all that, bare in mind that over doing it could potentially injure your hands, so be careful.

Keep It Slow

As you know, boogie woogie is normally played quite fast, sometimes very fast in fact, so a common mistake would be to try and instantly play at full speed.   In a word... Don't. After-all, if you haven't played something before then how can you expect to play it at full speed? Your brain can only absorb information so fast (remember, you are trying to programme it) so if you try and play too fast then you aren't going to properly absorb the information. Sure... you are still practicing, but it wont be as efficient. So it is good practice to initially play at a slower speed (whatever you can handle) until such a time as you feel you can speed it up – although this will come naturally. This is a more efficient form of practice and time is precious, make the most of it.

Don't Practice Mistakes

A mistake people make is that when they practice something and they make a mistake, they keep on practicing the same thing and making the same mistake. This is particularly a problem when trying to practice a piece at a speed you aren't quite ready for.   Why is this a problem you may ask? After-all, mistakes are why you practice. Let me explain.

When you practice something, you are programming your brain with a set of commands it needs to remember in order to play a piece of music.   If you continuously play a mistake over and over again, then you are essentially programming your brain to play that mistake. You (the conscious you) might know there's a mistake, but your unconscious computer programmed part doesn't know it's an error.

So when you know you have a mistake (a part you can't play properly) and you are continually making this mistake... stop, step back (not literally), go back to it with everything slowed down, analyse what is going on and practice what it was supposed to be, slowly, at a speed you can play without a problem. After a time you will then have mastered this part and you'll be able to put it back into the piece at its proper tempo.
In short, if the mistake doesn't go away easily, stop and work on it separately before you continue on.

Break It Down Into Sections

Something that many people do, is when they get a new piece of sheet music they try playing the piece from start to finish. Well sure, this is fine for a quick run through to see what you are working with, but there is a problem thereafter.

Many peoples idea of practicing a new piece (and we are talking sheet music here) is to continue to play it through from start to finish every-time they practice it. This isn't a particularly effective way to practice something new, it's fine once you know the piece and you are simply polishing it or refreshing your memory, but not when you first learn it.

It's generally considered far more efficient to break it down into sections. The size of these will vary depending on difficulty/ability. This might mean a single bar, or perhaps four bars, maybe the first page. But whatever the size, this gives you less to learn/take in at any one time and so less for your brain to try and accommodate at one time. This should be a far more effective method of learning a new piece of music.

How Many Pieces Should You Work On

How many different pieces or aspects of music should you work on at any one time? Well that will be different for different people, so I would recommend as many as you can handle. Personally if I spend too long on one piece of music at a time my brain switches off, obviously this isn't a very efficient use of time. So I always have several things that I am working on so I can switch between them. As long as you practice regularly this is fine, as each piece will get plenty of practice time. It also helps to keep your interest and enthusiasm up as you won't get tired of hearing the same thing over and over again.

Switching Subject During Practice

This is an interesting idea and is again to do with how the brain processes information. A study had shown that you get more efficient practice when you swap the subject matter (piece of music) often during a practice session.

The idea is this, when you play something new the first time your brain must adapt and create new pathways, but... if you continued to play the same small part over and over and over again, the part of your brain that learns new things essentially switches off and you are on a kind of auto pilot, and often any improvements you make are temporary.

As an example, many of you may have spent ages practicing something one day, going over and over it until you manage to get it right, but... the following day you try it again and you are nearly back to square one. Obviously your brain wasn't properly programmed.

So the theory is that if you work on a few bars of music, or practice a single scale, only go over them so many times (lets say ten as an example). This will have your brain initially struggling, trying to process this and make new pathways/connections. But after those ten runs over that section or scale, stop, change the piece you are working on to something new... what happens? Your brain is faced with something new again, so it will work to create new pathways yet again. Of course you will only work on this one so many times too (lets say ten again) before changing to yet another piece, (or section of the same song, or new scale, or whatever). You might have half a dozen things you are working on at once, continually swapping between them. This should keep your brain working harder, as it's being faced with something apparently new all the time, and so preventing it going into the auto pilot mode that can fool you into thinking you've cracked it. In short, it is supposed to speed up your intake of information. I hope that made sense.

It's an interesting theory, and if you look at it logically it does make a degree of sense. I have tried it myself, although it is hard to say for sure if it speeds up the learning process, but it certainly doesn't hurt, plus it has the benefit of keeping the practice session varied and so interesting.

Practice In Different Keys

This is more specific to boogie woogie, although it is also an issue if you play the blues. There are twelve keys (If you count F♯ as the same as G♭, which in practical terms it is). It is common for people to only play in C when they start out. This is absolutely fine. After-all, the piano is designed to work with the key of C, it is the piano key and most of the examples in this book are in the key of C (for ease and simplicity).

The problem that can come though is when you don't move away from the key of C. This leaves you unable to play effectively in other keys, which can become quite limiting. I made this mistake when I was younger, becoming proficient in C but not so in other keys and it took me sometime to rectify this. So, once you've got the basics, don't delay, start playing what you know in other keys.

Some keys are far more common and popular than others of course, who plays boogie in the key of B for example? not many people perhaps. But after C I'd suggest the key of G then maybe the key of F, E♭ has a good sound and I quite like playing in A myself. E is a good one if you want to play in bands, as guitarists like the key of E. A good idea is to listen to lots of recordings, this will soon show you what keys are in popular use and so give you an idea of what keys to concentrate on.

Transposing

This is a vital skill to master if you intend to play in different keys, fortunately the basic idea is relatively simple, especially with this form of music.

We are generally speaking (in a basic boogie) only dealing with three chords. Rather than think of these in terms of transposing up and down, it is far better to just memorise the chords that fit the corresponding key you are to play in. All you need to know is the major scale of each key and you can work out what chords the I, IV and V are. Or... you could use the chart shown below as a short cut. You will of course soon learn and remember these and they'll soon become second nature.

CHORDS FOR CORRESPONDING KEY

KEY	I CHORD	IV CHORD	V CHORD
A	A	D	E
B♭	B♭	E♭	F
B	B	E	G♭
C	C	F	G
D♭	D♭	G♭	A♭
D	D	G	A
E♭	E♭	A♭	B♭
E	E	A	B
F	F	B♭	C
G♭	G♭	B	D♭
G	G	C	D
A♭	A♭	D♭	E♭

Transposing

Once you know the chords you are dealing with, you can then work out how to transpose whatever bass line you wish to work with.

NOTE

Although with twelve possible keys (although in reality you probably won't work with them all) you have thirty-six possible combinations of chords, remember that most of these are repeated. There are still only twelve keys/chords to worry about.

As an example...   lets assume you can play in C but wish to play in G.

Instead of the chords C, F and G, you are now faced with the chords G, C and D, but notice that the only extra chord/scale you may not be familiar with is... D.   The other two.. C and G you would already have learnt.

So now you know what chords you a using for your new key, but how do you transpose a riff you know in C to D? (for example).

First... looking at the keyboard (or using your head) count how many semi-tones there are from one note to the other, or look on the sheet music if available.

Example

As you can see, the distance between these two notes is two semi-tones.
With this information you can then transpose a riff accordingly.

(NOTE)

A semi-tone is the distance between one note, or one key on the piano
keyboard (including black and white).

Example. 1

This example bass pattern consists of the notes C, G and A

Counting up two semi-tones from these will give you.... D, A and B, which creates
the same pattern in D (shown below)

Example. 2

To transpose from C to F. Count the semi-tones between the notes, this will show you
that they are five semi-tones apart (as shown in example below).

Therefore, to change any pattern/riff from C to F requires each individual note to be
raised by five semi-tones.

So this pattern in C....

Becomes the same pattern in F (all notes being five semi-tones higher).

That is the basis of transposing a riff into different keys. There aren't any short cuts, magic formulas or special skills involved, becoming proficient is merely a matter of practice. The more you try this, the easier and quicker it becomes, as you will come to recognise patterns and automatically have an idea of how they will appear in another key.

One tip is to look for the key points of a riff

Examples

1) Starting point.

Does the riff start on the root, the third or maybe the fifth?
Knowing this means you'll know where to start in the new key, no transposing required.

2) Look for a chord.

Look at the riff, does it contain or consist of a chord you recognise?
If so, you can then easily take this information and use it to play or at least help form the riff in the new key.

3) Does it follow a single scale.

Does the riff directly follow one of the scales you know?
If so, then you will be able to use the corresponding scale of the new key, and form the same riff in the new key using the corresponding scale.

4) Recognise intervals

Does the riff consist of intervals you recognise, thirds, fifths, sixths, maybe octaves?
If so, you can just use your knowledge of the new key and easily recreate the riff, knowing the same intervals in the different key.

5) Recognise specific notes

Look at the riff you want to transpose, does is use flattened thirds, flattened fifths, ninths?
Does it perhaps have grace notes sliding from the minor third to the third?
You can use these clues (which can be visual too) to help you find the correct notes in the new key. With practice this can become second nature.

Playing By Ear

Written notation from books, magazines or the internet is a great way of getting started when learning a new style of music. These can teach the basics, like how the music is structured and give you examples of chord progressions and some riffs that may be employed. But after awhile you will need to go beyond this, and the best way to really get to know a style of music is to learn from listening directly to the masters and then copy them. This is what anyone who is half-way any good has done at some point in their life, in-fact some of the best players learned only by doing this and have no music reading skills what-so-ever.

If you are trying to learn a new style of music, you should be listening to it all the time, as this allows you to absorb the sound and the feel of the music. In order to improvise well you need the music to be internalized, so it can come out naturally, almost instinctual. And for that to happen you must listen to the music as often as possible, it really makes a big difference. After-all, how can you improvise if you can't hear something in your head, listening to boogie woogie will (without even knowing it) give you a library of material to use.

So once you have the basic skills and can knock out some good old boogie woogie, the way to really push yourself further is to listen to the best of the best, work out what they are playing and then try and recreate what they do. This is THE way to go.
There are a few ways to go about this, and those of you who are just starting out should consider yourselves fortunate, as some of the technology available today makes this so much easier than when I first started out doing this.

When I first tried doing this, I used to listen to tapes, or CD's and constantly had to stop and rewind, stop and rewind, trying to catch what was happening at any specific point. Anyone who has done this will know how hard it is. One step easier than that was watching a live performance on VHS (do you remember video tape?) as you would get an occasional view of the keyboard - which helped endlessly - although it was rare I would get a recording to watch. Fortunately technology has moved on and it's easier these days, but I stress easier, not easy, as it's still a tricky time consuming exercise, but with practice it does become easier.

Whatever your form of media, one thing is the same, you must be sitting at a piano/keyboard. In the old days you might have had a record player next to the piano, or perhaps a tape player sitting on top. These days it's more likely to be a laptop, or a tablet, maybe even your mobile phone. Whatever your choice, set it within easy reach, I find a large tablet is ideal, as you can place it on the music rest of the piano.

Tips/Advice

I'm sure people probably approach this slightly differently, but this is how I tend to go about it. In some respects boogie woogie is easier for this, as you don't have as many chord changes to worry about, but regardless the general idea is simple.

1) Working out the key.

This is the first step, again, due to boogie woogie having a relatively simple chord structure it is quite easy to do. After listening to the piece you will be able to identify what the I, IV and V chords are, so from there it's easy to match the key by trying it out on the keyboard. Just try different notes until you find a match that's in key, simple.

2) Working Out The Bass

Work on the left and right hands separately. Boogie woogie generally consists of a repeating pattern on the left-hand, so to get the basic idea of what is being played is not too bad (relatively). You know the key it's in, so you'll know the scales and so the notes that are available to you. One step at a time, just try notes out and see if you can find a match, there's no magic formula, it's very much trial and error. The more musical knowledge you have and the more practice at this you have the easier it becomes. After time, you will hear something and from experience you will roughly know the basis of what is being played.

3) Working Out The Right-Hand

Again, this is trial and error, and experience makes this easier. One step is to match the chords being played. Is it a 7th, 6th, 13th ...? Once you know, this gives you further clues as to what notes will work. Does what the pianist plays sound familiar? Much of boogie is variations of other riffs you may already know, if this is the case then try what you know but modify it in an attempt to match the recording.
Come close? But can't quite find it?
Well there are only so many notes so don't become disheartened, keep playing around possible combinations, it's there somewhere, they may be a professional legend but they still only have twelve notes to an octave the same as you.

4) Play Along

Once you have a rough idea of what they are doing, try it out, play along with the recording and see if it's somewhere near. If they are doing something completely different to what you first thought, this will highlight it. Playing along to a recording is quite a good technique anyway, as it helps with timing and the feel of the music.

5) Make a Note

If you are able, I would suggest making a note of what you have worked out. It is extremely annoying to spend hours working out some master piece, only to forget most of it because you've not played it for awhile. This doesn't necessarily have to be a perfect note for note transcription, but a few notes to jog your memory is fine.

Different Media Options/Approaches

1) CD's/Tapes/Records

This could be considered the old school way, and is perhaps the hardest. Having to rewind constantly is a tricky and frustrating thing. Last resort only these days.

2) MP3

A better option is to convert any old boogie woogie songs into MP3's. This then allows you to place either a laptop on top of your piano, or better still place a mobile phone or tablet on the music rest (the larger the better). This is the best option in my opinion. You will find it far easier to stop, start and rewind the music you are learning this way. Having a touch screen directly in front of you is a far better option than having a clumsy CD or tape player.

3) Video

This is potentially the best way to go about it, if possible. Being able to see what the pianist is playing is worth its weight in gold, after-all, the piano is quite a visual instrument with the arrangement of the keys allowing you to see what is being played.

The best way of finding material to work from these days has got to be YouTube. Obviously video recordings of the old legends of boogie woogie are an extremely rare thing, and even of you find some old footage it wont be of good enough quality to be of much use. But that's fine, as there are many modern pianists who have been recorded playing live, often with the camera right over the keyboard (at least some of the time). You can often find a version of an old classic, or a more modern song that you can both listen to and watch. This combination speeds up the process ten fold, as if you can't quite work out what is being played from the music, a few visual clues can help put you back on the right track.

Another trick you can do here, is that YouTube (depending on the device) allows you to slow the video down. With fast music like boogie woogie... I would think the advantages of this were quite obvious.

4) DAW's (Digital Audio Workstations)

This won't be of use to many pianists, but if you're into modern digital technology (I have it and use it, although I much prefer to just play a nice acoustic piano), then you will know what I mean by a DAW. If you are so equipped... this is something I have done in the past.   If you have a recording you want to work out (and it's not available on YouTube) then record it into the DAW software (or import it if it's already a file on a PC), and then you will have the song available to manipulate. You can easily set up a loop (an A to B repeat) of the section you are working on, making it far easier.   Or you can (depending on the software) slow the music down to a more suitable tempo where you can catch what is going on. A very useful tool.

Bass Line 1
12 Keys

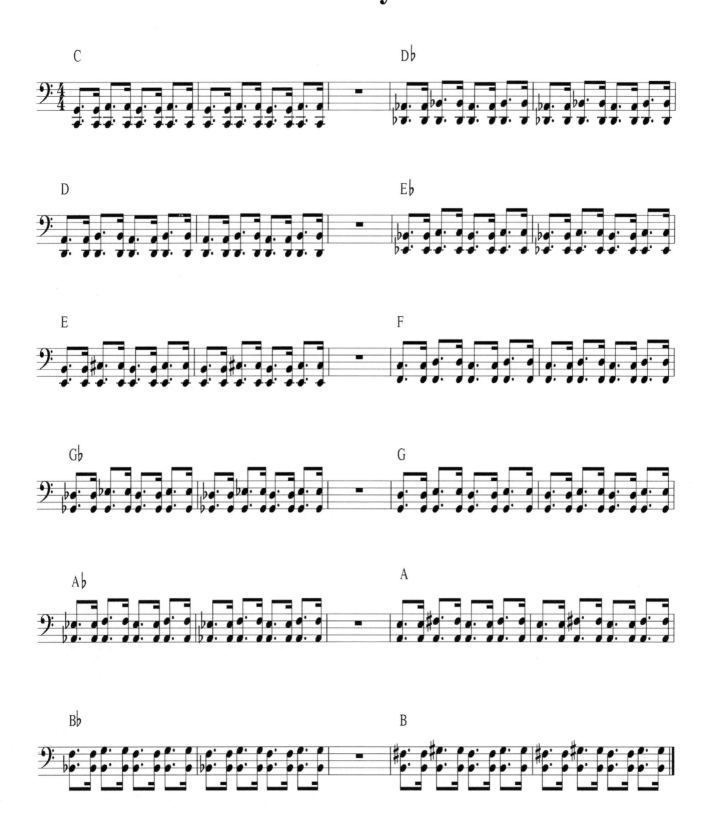

Bass Line 2
12 Keys

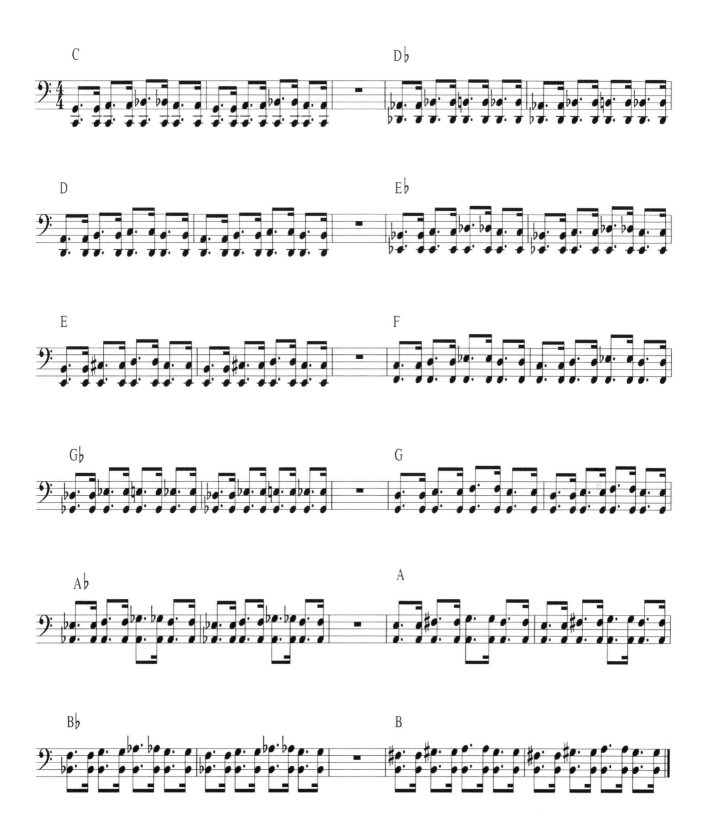

Bass Line 3
12 Keys

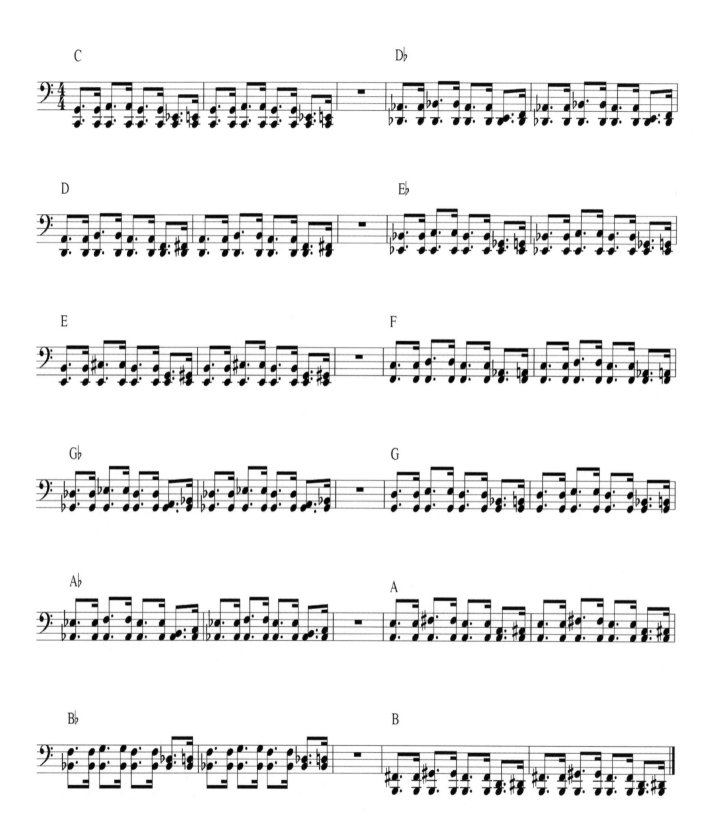

Bass Line 4
12 Keys

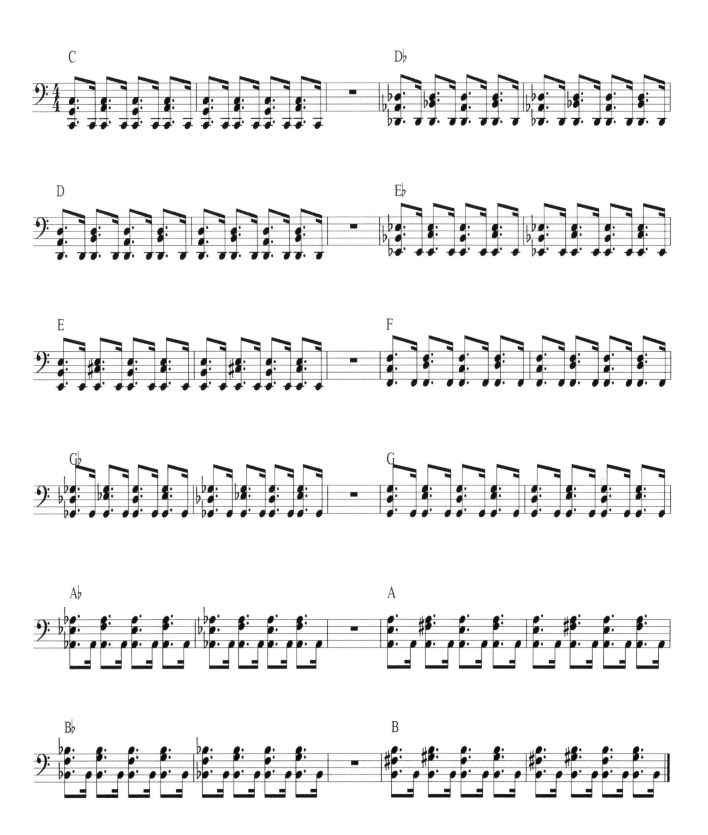

Bass Line 5
12 Keys

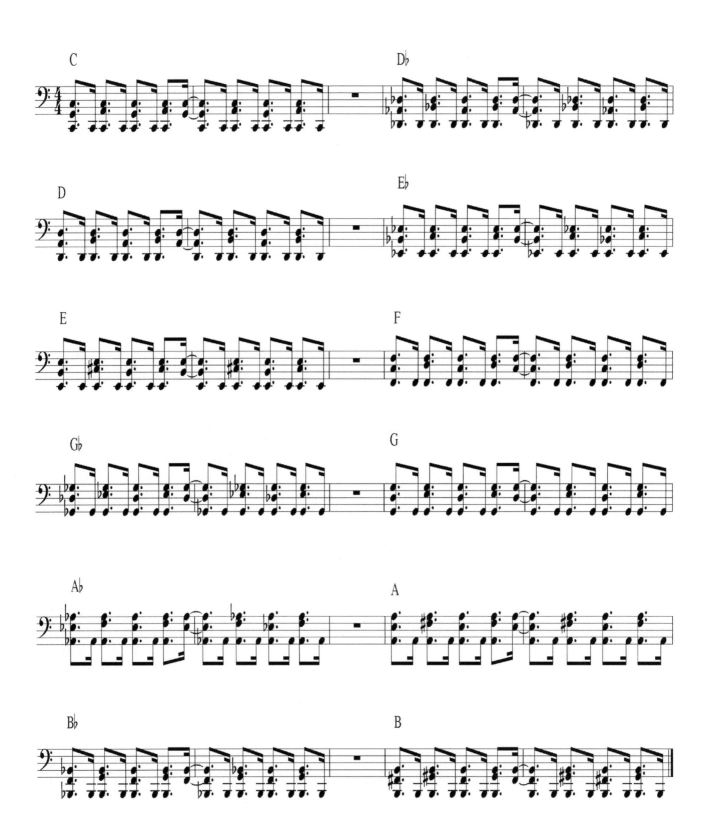

Bass Line 6
12 Keys

Bass Line 7
12 Keys

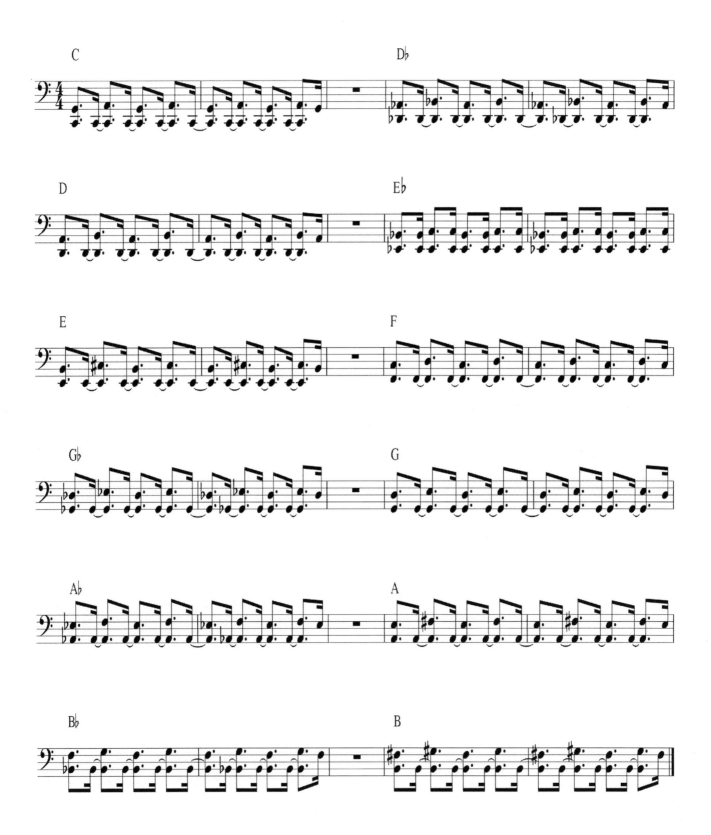

194

Bass Line 8
12 Keys

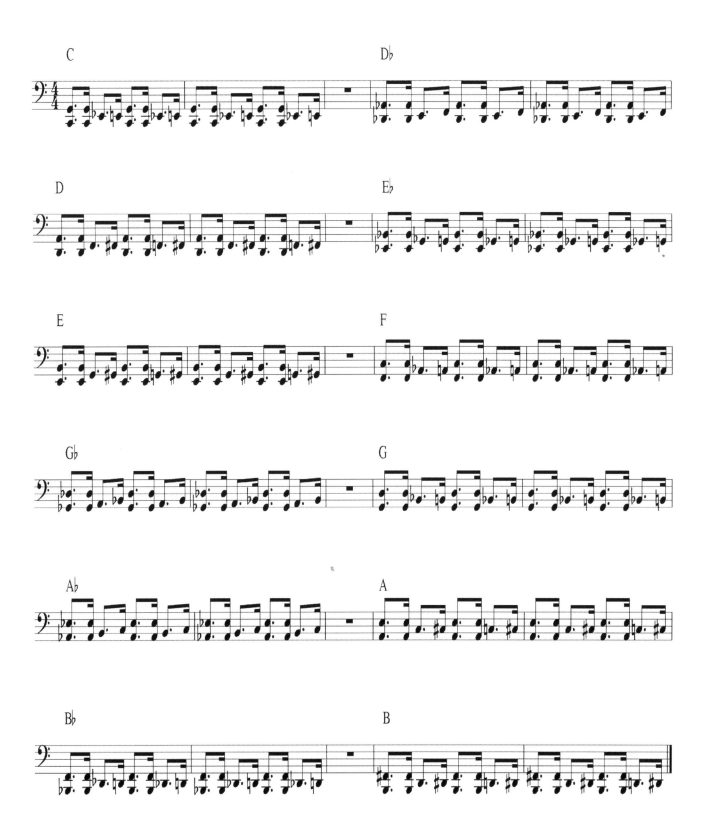

Bass Line 9
12 Keys

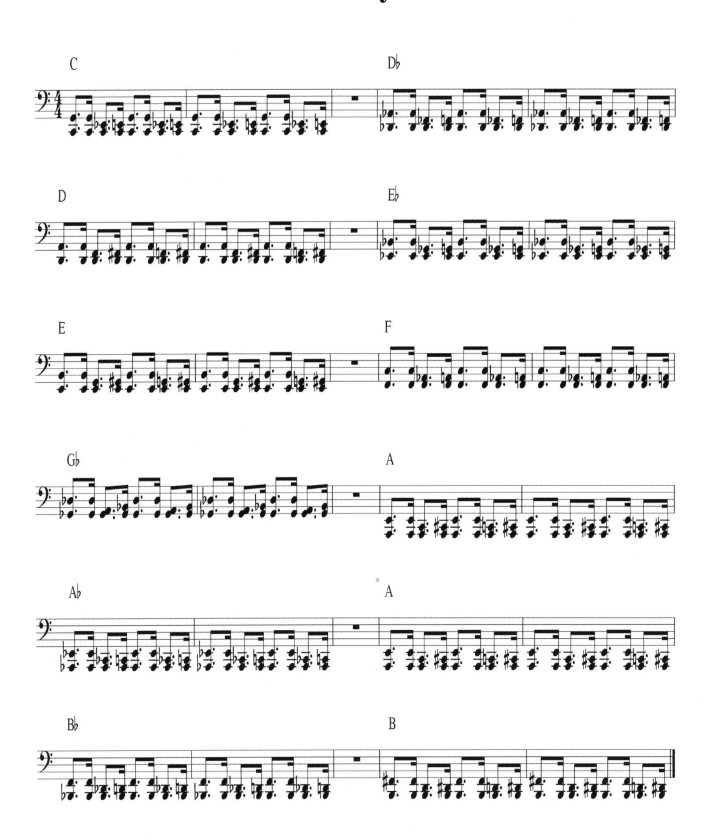

Bass Line 10
12 Keys

Bass Line 11
12 Keys

Bass Line 12
12 Keys

Bass Line 13
12 Keys

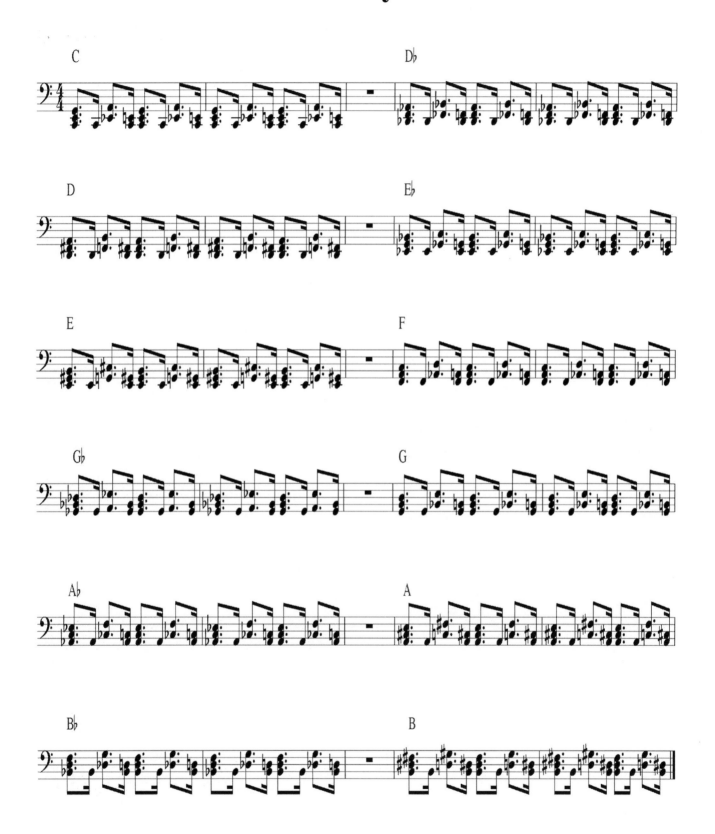

Bass Line 14
12 Keys

Bass Line 15
12 Keys

Bass Line 16
12 Keys

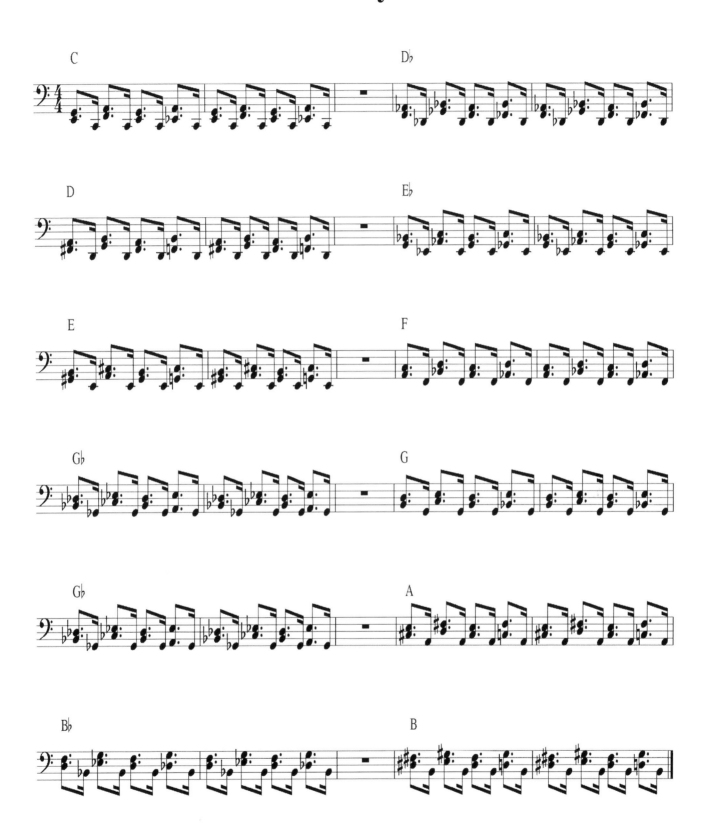

Bass Line 17
12 Keys

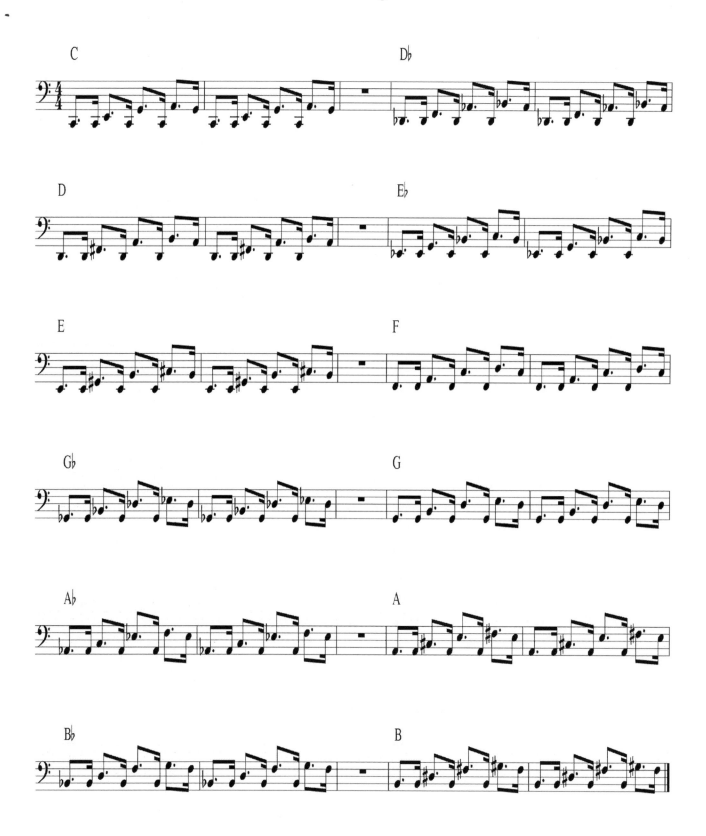

Bass Line 18
12 Keys

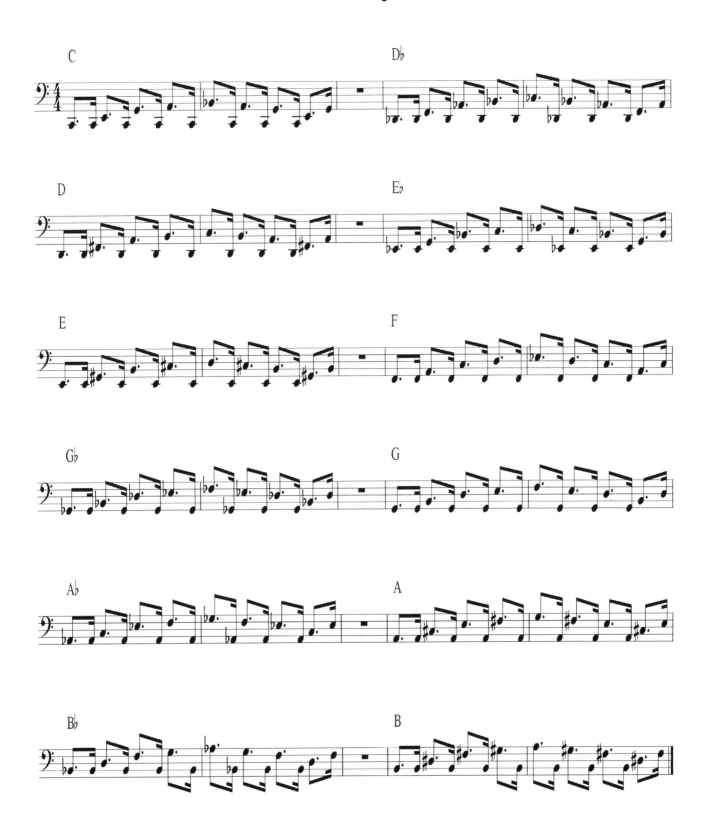

Bass Line 19
12 Keys

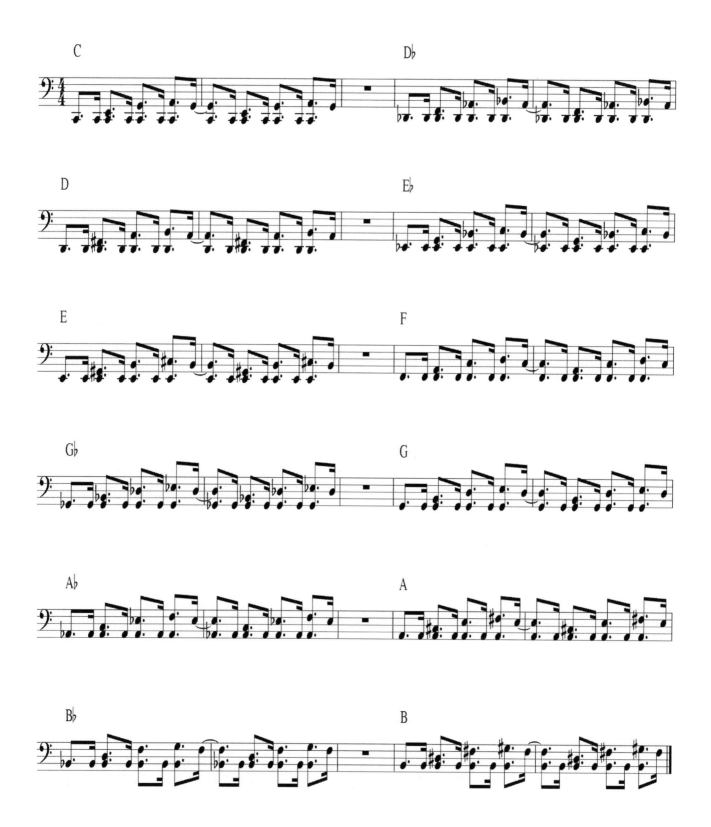

Bass Line 20
12 Keys

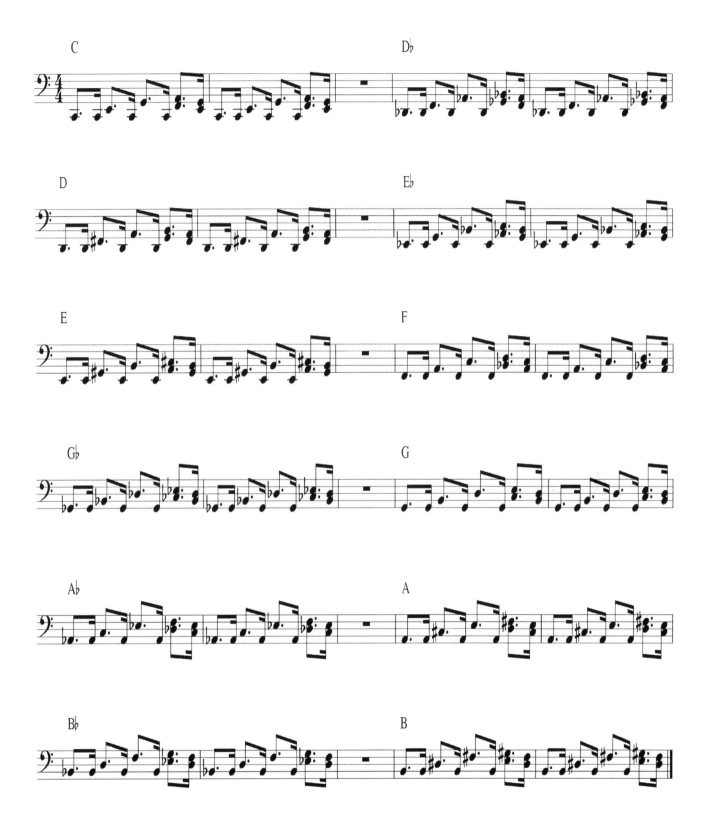

Bass Line 21
12 Keys

Bass Line 22
12 Keys

Bass Line 23
12 Keys

Bass Line 24
12 Keys

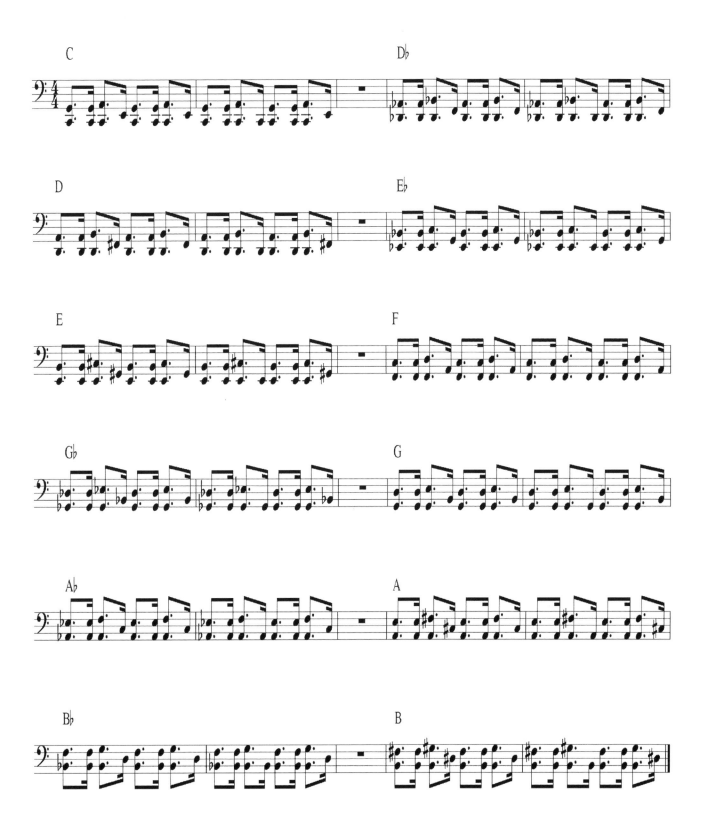

Bass Line 25
12 Keys

Bass Line 26
12 Keys

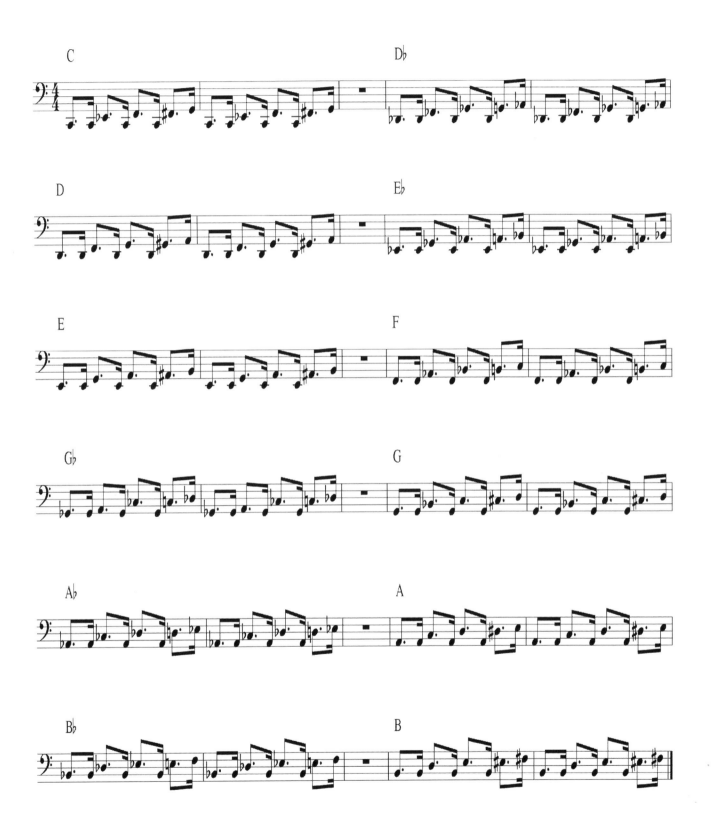

Bass Line 27
12 Keys

Bass Line 28
12 Keys

Bass Line 29
12 Keys

Bass Line 30
12 Keys

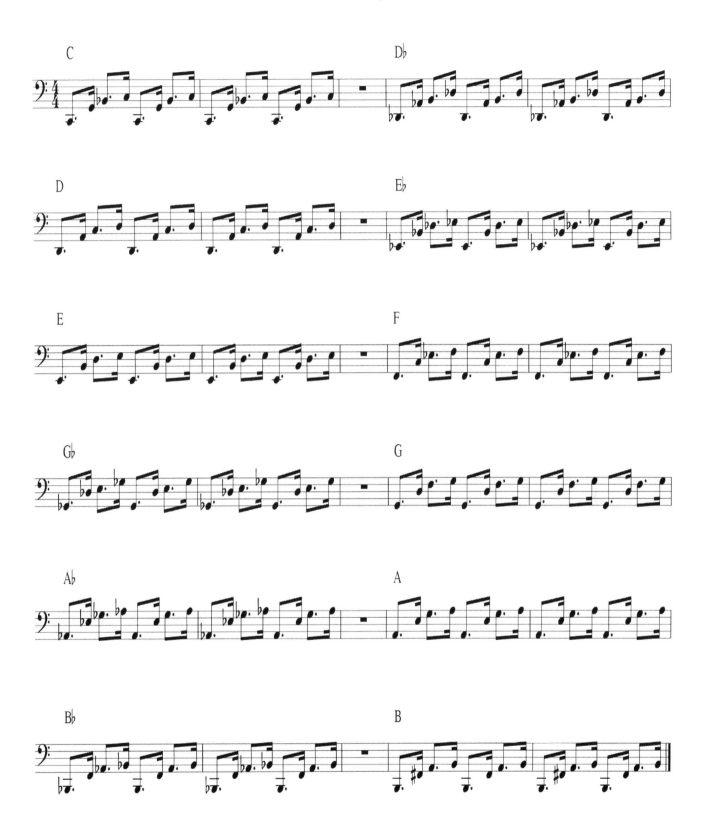

Bass Line 31
12 Keys

Bass Line 32
12 Keys

Bass Line 33
12 Keys

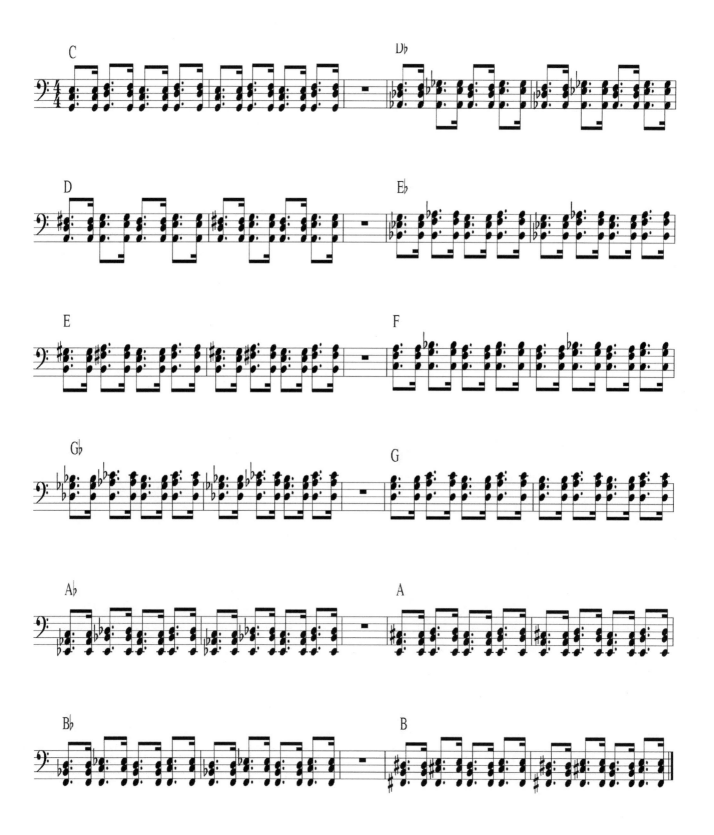

Bass Line 34
12 Keys

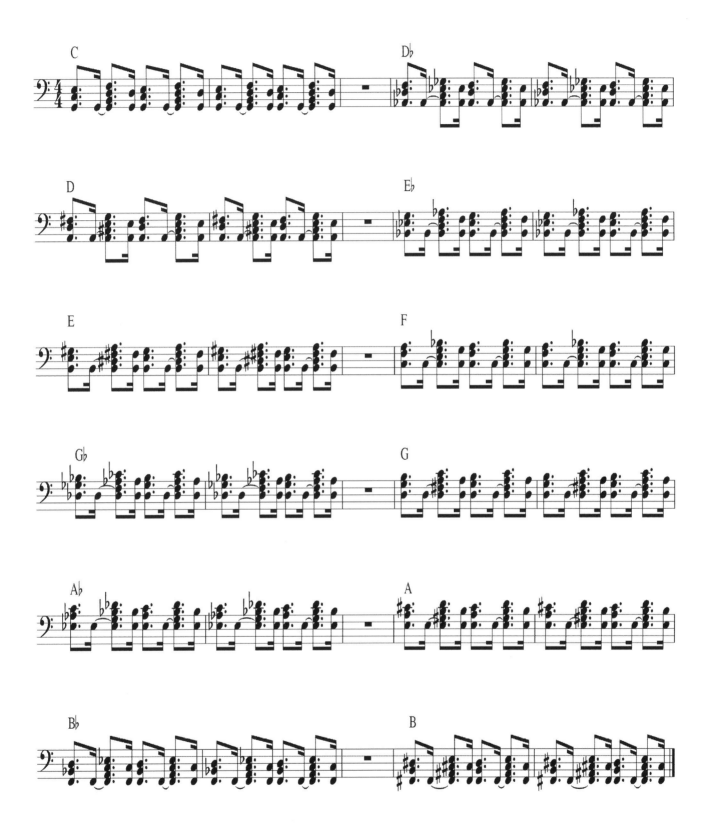

Bass Line 35
12 Keys

Bass Line 36
12 Keys

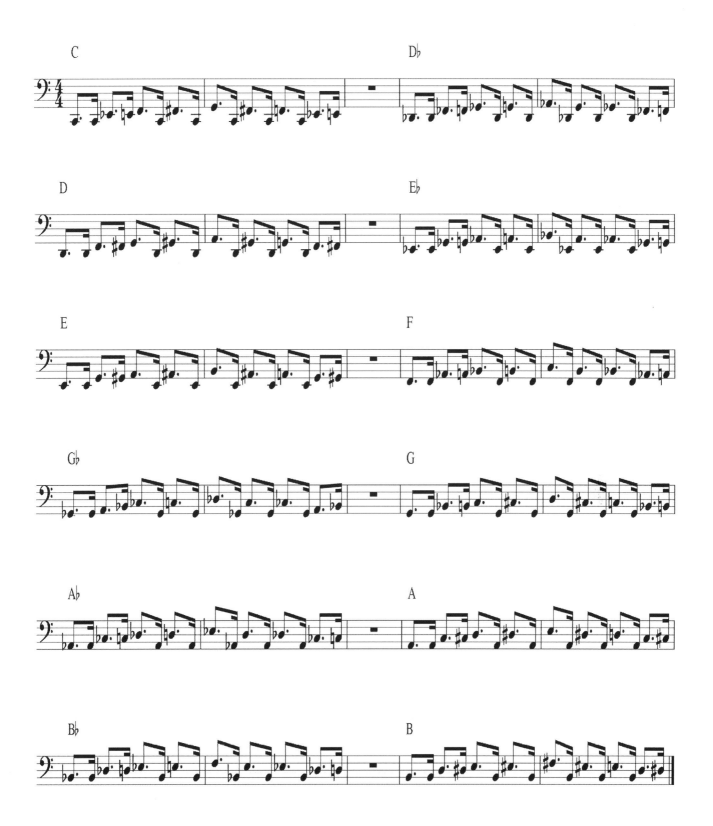

Bass Line 37
12 Keys

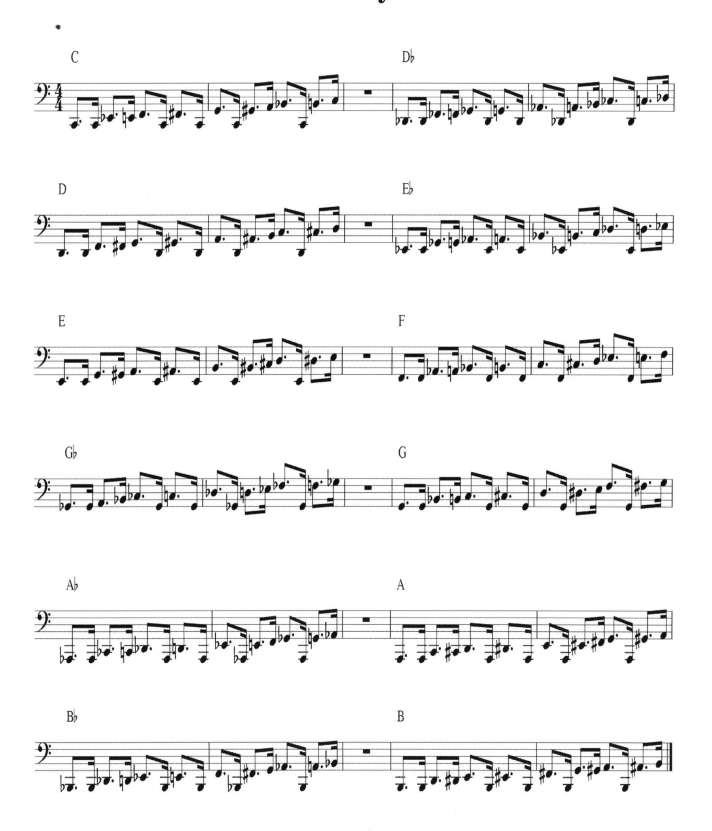

Further Reading

HISTORICAL

If you are interested in the history of boogie woogie, then I would recommend trying...
'A Left Hand Like God' by Peter J. Silvester. (1988)
This is a very in depth look at the history of the music. A few editions have been printed, the later revision (2009) is said to also cover later (modern) years.

PIANO TUITION BOOKS

There are a hand-full of tuition books currently available (at the time of writing) to help you learn boogie woogie piano.

Boogie Woogie Piano – fast forward series	*by Bill Worall*
Hal Leonard Keyboard Styles series	*by Todd Lowry*
Boogie Woogie For Beginners	*Hal Leonard Corp*
How To Play Boogie Woogie Piano	*by Dave Rubin*
Boogie Woogie Hanon	*by Leo Alfassy*
Discovering Boogie & Blues Piano	*by Wolfgang Wierzyk*
How To Play Boogie-Woogie Piano	*by Frank Booth*

OTHER BOOKS

There aren't that many song books available, although you may find something suitable in your local music shop. For many songs - especially the classic songs - the internet is probably best source.

The Real Blues'n Boogie Buch   *by Wiedermann.*
This isn't published in English sadly, but don't let that put you off, as the music within is of a good quality. In-fact, one of my favourite up and coming pianists has used this book.

Six Blues Roots Pianists   *by Eric Kriss*
This is out of print, but available second-hand or on the Kindle - if you must.

Boogie Woogie: Piano solos   *by Axel Zwingenberger*
This is also sadly out of print, but it does appear second hand from time to time.
This consists of note for note transcriptions of one of Zwingenberger's albums, so the actual content is extremely authentic, rather than being the typical simplified fare.

Luca Sestak : Favorites   by Luca Sestak
This is a note for note transcription of five songs from Luca's second album, which, incidentally I would definitely recommend.

Dr. John Teaches New Orleans Piano : Vol.1   by Dr. John   (Hal Leonard)
This is the first in a series of three books.
Although he's not solely a boogie woogie pianist... Vol.1 particularly, focuses more on boogie than anything else. Comes with a CD of him playing the pieces.   Plus it's Dr. John, what more could you ask for.

Tuition Dvd's

Tutorial video's on many styles of music have been around for years. Now, although the entire world seems to be moving online these days, there are still some that you might want to try.

Dr. John Teaches New Orleans Piano. Vol.1 , Vol.2, Vol.3.
This is three separate DVD's that accompany the book in the same series. It is Dr. John himself teaching you , with a full view of the piano keyboard.

The Piano Styles Of Dr. John
This is a double DVD of Dr. John at the piano, going over around 37 songs.
Certainly a good learning tool, plus its good to see him play.

Johnnie Johnson : Sessions with a Legend
Although Johnnie Johnson is known for blues/rock, his basis is very much boogie woogie.
If you like his music, then I would recommend this DVD.

Chuck Leavell Piano Instruction Vol.1
Again, Chuck isn't strictly a boogie woogie pianist, but he does cover it in one section, plus the blues sections will transfer over nicely to boogie. Nicely done, a shame Vol.2 never appeared.

Boogie Woogie Pianists

This is by no means a complete list, but rather a list of those that I have come across myself. It may give you a starting point of possible pianists to investigate further. Some are solely boogie woogie pianists, where as others cover a more diverse range of styles, but all of them are a great source to learn from.

EARLY DAYS

Albert Ammons	(1907-1949)	Cow Cow Davenport	(1894-1955)
Blind John Davis	(1913-1985)	Champion Jack Dupree	(1908-1992)
William Ezall	(1892-1963	Pete Johnson	(1904-1967)
Meade Lux Lewis	(1905-1964)	Little Willie Littlefield	(1931-2013)
Cripple Clarence Lofton	(1887-1957)	Little Brother Montgomery	(1906-1085)
Memphis Slim	(1915-1988)	Sammy Price	(1908-1992)
Clarence Pinetop Smith	(1904-1929)	Speckled Red	(1892-1973)
Roosevelt Sykes	(1906-1983)	Jimmy Yancy	(1898-1951)

MID YEARS

Dr. John (Mac Rebenack)	(1940)	Neville Dickie	(1937)
Johnnie Johnson	(1924-2005)	Bob Hall	(1942)
Oscar Peterson	(1925-2007)	Bob Seeley	(c1930)
Huey 'piano' Smith	(1934)	Otis Spann	(1930-1970)
Kenny Wayne	(1944)	Mitch Woods	(1951)
Vince Weber	(1953)	Axel Zwingenberger	(1955)

MODERN & NEWCOMERS

Chris Conz	(1985)	Chase Garret	(1989)
Henri Herbert	(1985)	Jools Holland	(1958)
Lasse Jensen	(1991)	Eeco Rijken Rapp	(1983)
Luca Sestak	(1995)	Ben Toury	(c1983)
Paddy Milner	(1980)	Ben Waters	(1974)
Silvan Zingg	(1973)		

(Apologies for any discrepancies)

Tyler music.co.uk

For further piano tuition books and a range of manuscript paper
visit our website at...

www.tylermusic.co.uk

Sign up for the newsletter for updates on new releases and
events regarding blues and boogie-woogie piano.

Printed in Poland
by Amazon Fulfillment
Poland Sp. z o.o., Wrocław

51459639R00137